A Time with Our Children
Year C

A Time with Our Children

Stories for Use in Worship
Year C

Dianne E. Deming

United Church Press
Cleveland, Ohio

United Church Press, Cleveland, Ohio 44115

Printed in the United States of America
The paper used in this publication is acid free and meets the minimum requirements of American National Standards for Information Sciences-Permanence of Paper for Printed Library Materials, ANSI Z39.48—1984

98 97 96 95 94 93   5 4 3 2 1

Library of Congress Cataloging-in-Publication Data
Deming, Dianne E.
   A time with our children.
   Includes indexes.
   Contents: [1] Year A   [3] Year C.
   1. Children's sermons. 2. Church year sermons.
I. Title.
BV4315.D422 1992   252'.53   92-31638
ISBN 0-8298-0941-4 (year A : alk. paper)
ISBN 0-8298-0953-8 (year C)

Dedicated to the children of
The United Presbyterian Church
Fort Morgan, Colorado

Contents

Introduction

The children's sermon is a relatively new component within the context of formal worship. Yet sharing the faith with the next generation has been an important priority since the time of Abraham and Sarah. Sharing our faith with the youngest members of the church family is what the children's sermon should be about. This understanding of why we include a specific time with our children in worship leads to two presuppositions.

The children's sermon should first and foremost be for children. This seems fairly obvious, yet too often this time is used as an additional opportunity for the pastor to get his or her point across to the adults of the congregation. If we believe the children's story is for children, then it needs to be understandable and interesting from a child's point of view.

Having said this, we must also remember that the most important benefit children receive from their special time in worship is the underlying message that they are valued and loved by God and their church. This cannot happen if the children's sermon is used as the comic relief portion of the service, for the entertainment of the adults.

A four-year-old boy sat with his mother and father in church until it was time for the children's story. He went to the front and sat on the chancel steps with the other boys and girls. The associate pastor began by asking the children a question. The little boy shouted out his earnest answer with enthusiasm. The congregation broke out laughing. The little boy didn't answer any more questions. When he returned to his pew he said to his mother, "Let's not come here any more."

We, as storytellers, cannot control a congregation's reaction. But we can try our best not to set children up to be embarrassed. As the storyteller, you can also help soften the blow of a situation like the one described above by taking the child's answer seriously yourself. Respond to the children and their answers with respect, letting them know that you appreciate what they've said.

Both of these presuppositions can be fulfilled if we listen to what we say and how we interact with the children from a child's point of view. This does not mean a compromise of theological integrity. On the contrary, the same thought and care that go into the twenty-minute message need to be applied to the children's sermon. It has been my aim to accomplish these goals with the stories you will find within these pages.

Jesus understood the power of a good story. He also knew the precious value of children, not because they are "the church of the future," but because they are the church of the present. "Let the children come to me and do not stop them, because the Kingdom of heaven belongs to such as these" (Matthew 19:14, TEV).

As we do our best to communicate the gospel to the children God has entrusted to our care, let us be learners as well as teachers, catching glimpses of God's kingdom in the faces of those gathered around us.

How to Use This Book

The stories in this book are based on the scripture readings from the *Common Lectionary* (Cycle C). There are also a topical and a scriptural index for those who do not follow the lectionary.

Several of the stories call for the use of a flannel board and flannel-board figures. These figures, with instructions on how to prepare them and the board, are found in the Appendix at the back of this book.

Finally, I encourage you to take these stories and make them your own. Tell them in your own words, add personal anecdotes that will enhance your message, change them in any way that will make them more effective for you to tell. And may the grace of God be with you.

Acknowledgments

The publication of this book represents the fulfillment of a dream I've held for many years. This dream could not have been achieved, however, but by the grace of God and the support of many people, several of whom I would like to recognize here.

First, I would like to thank my parents, Leonard and Anne Jones, who taught me by their example how rich a life of faith could be and laid the groundwork for my own faith journey. I would like to thank my husband, Frank, for the loving support without which this book probably would not have been written, and for several of the story ideas found herein. Thank you also to my sister, Kathy Onnen, for her love and support throughout this project and always.

Thank you to Robert Bielenberg, pastor of the United Presbyterian Church of Fort Morgan, Colorado for teaching me what being a pastor is all about. Thank you to Jack Purdy, former editor of the Presbyterian and Reformed Educational Ministry resources, for giving me my first opportunity to write for publication.

Many thanks to Barbara Withers, my editor, for taking a chance on a little-published author and for all of her helpfulness, and to the rest of the staff at The Pilgrim Press.

Finally, thank you to the children in my life. To the boys and girls of the United Presbyterian Church of Fort Morgan, thank you for being my friends and for allowing me to share the gospel with you nearly every Sunday for seven years. And to my son, Scott, thank you for reminding me what it's like to be a child.

Season of Advent

Psalm 25:1–10

The Waiting Game

Prop Needed

Your church's Advent wreath (If your church doesn't have an Advent wreath, you may use an Advent calendar. These are available through most religious bookstores and stationery/gift shops.)

The Message

Have any of you ever had to wait for something, and it seemed like forever until that something finally came? Do you think it's hard to wait for cookies to come out of the oven, for example? They smell so good, you can almost taste them, but you have to wait until they're baked and cooled before you can eat any. How about a trip to the park, or to Grandma's, or to someplace like Disneyland? Is it hard to wait for these things? What else is hard to wait for? *(Encourage the children to respond.)*

How many of you think it's hard to wait for Christmas? I do, too. The church also understands how difficult it is to wait for Christmas. It has even given the four weeks before Christmas a special name. We call these four weeks of waiting *Advent.* Can you say that? Advent. The word *Advent* means "arrival" or "coming." During the four weeks of Advent, we wait for the coming of Jesus on his birthday, Christmas.

Sometimes it helps us wait for things if we do something while we're waiting. While we're waiting for cookies, we might help clean up the dishes. In the church, we do something that helps us wait for Christmas. We use an Advent wreath. Let me show it to you. Come on over here. *(If possible, gather around the wreath or stand in a spot where all can see it.)*

You see that the wreath has four candles around the outside, forming a circle, and one white candle in the center. *(Fully describe your church's wreath—any words on it, etc.)* Each Sunday between now and Christmas, a candle will be lit on the Advent wreath. Some of you may be helping to light these candles with your families *(if applicable.)* This is the First Sunday of Advent, and so one candle will be *(or is)* lit. Next Sunday there will be two, the next Sunday three, and finally four candles will be lit on the wreath. The candle in the middle is called the Christ candle. It is lit on Christmas Eve. So when you come to church, and all of the candles are lit, you will know the next day is Christmas—the day we've all been waiting for!

Let's pray. Dear God, sometimes waiting for something special can be so hard—especially waiting for something as special as the birthday of your child, Jesus. May we find helpful things to do while we're waiting. In Jesus' name we pray. Amen.

Get Ready . . .

Props Needed
Several Christmas ornaments, one representing a crèche

The Message
Good morning, boys and girls. How many candles are lit on the Advent wreath this morning? Two! *(Omit if your wreath isn't lit until later in the service.)* Today is the Second Sunday of Advent. We're another week closer to Christmas, aren't we?

Remember, last week we talked about Advent as being four weeks of waiting. Advent is also four weeks of preparation, or getting ready, for Christmas. Have you and your family started to get ready? What kinds of things do we do to get ready, or prepare, for Christmas? *(Encourage children to respond. Of course, there will be many Santa-related answers, but that's okay. Listen to all answers without critiquing them.)*

One of the things I like to do to get ready for Christmas is put up the Christmas tree. Have any of your families put up a tree yet? I have brought a few ornaments from my tree for you to see this morning. *(Show the children the ornaments, excluding the crèche. If possible, it would be good to have a variety, including a miniature Santa. You might share any stories or history related to the ornaments.)*

I have a question for you now. Why do we do all these things? Why is it that every year we bake cookies, give presents, have special parties, decorate our homes, send cards, decorate trees, sing carols, have a church pageant—why do we do these things? What is the big deal? *(Wait for answers.)*

We do all these things because on Christmas Jesus was born!

We do all these special things at Christmastime because Jesus is coming, not because Santa is coming! In fact, Santa comes to help us celebrate Jesus' birthday.

I have saved the best Christmas tree ornament to show you last. Can you tell me what it is? That's right—it's a tiny nativity scene, or crèche. Can you see Joseph and Mary? And there's the baby Jesus in the manger. I like this ornament because it helps me to remember the *most* wonderful thing about Christmas. When I see this ornament hanging on my tree, I remember that God loves each of us so much, that God sent the son, Jesus, into the world. And that's why Christmas is such a big deal!

Let's pray. Dear God, we thank you for the things that make Christmas so special. Help us to remember what the big deal is all about—the birth of Jesus. We love you, too, God. Amen.

Get Set . . .

Prop Needed
A picture of your cousin, or of two people who are cousins

The Message
Hi, everybody. I have a picture to show you this morning. This is a picture of my cousin. Her name is Mary Smith, and she lives in Denver, Colorado. Her mother and my mother are sisters, which makes Mary and me cousins. How many of you have cousins?

Today I want to tell you about Jesus' cousin. He was about six months older than Jesus, and his name was John. When both men were thirty years old, God gave each of them very important work to do. Jesus was sent by God. His job was to help the people know God and to understand how much God loved them. John's work was to help the people get ready for the one God had sent, who was Jesus.

You see, Jesus was born that first Christmas, and he grew up just as we grow up. First he was a baby, then a little child, then a big kid, until finally he grew up to be an adult. While Jesus was growing up very few people realized how special he was. They didn't know he was sent by God for a special reason—to teach the people about God's love. They thought he was just another boy from Nazareth, who became a carpenter like his dad.

The people had been waiting for years and years for God to send someone. But they had no idea that that one was Jesus. John, then, was to help the people get used to the idea that God's Chosen One had come. He was to help get them ready for the special person God sent to them.

John told the people, "Get ready! God's Chosen One is coming!" The people asked John, "What should we do?" John told them, "Share what you have with others. Don't cheat people. Be honest and kind to each other."

John said that people needed to get ready for Jesus on the inside, and not just on the outside. We need to get ready for Jesus on the inside, and not just on the outside, too. We need to prepare our hearts, and not just our homes, for Christmas.

How do we prepare our hearts for Jesus' arrival at Christmas? We can follow John's advice. We can share what we have with others. Perhaps you have an older neighbor who is alone. You could make that person a special Christmas card or give him or her some of the cookies you've baked. Maybe while you're out shopping, you could buy an extra toy to give to someone who doesn't have much to play with. You can try extra hard to be kind to your brothers and sisters or do extra chores without being asked. All of these things show that we care about other people. Caring for others is one way we show Jesus we love him—at Christmas and all through the year.

Let's pray. Loving God, we thank you for sending us Jesus. Help us to prepare our hearts, as well as our homes, to receive him. In Jesus' name we pray. Amen.

Go!

Props Needed
A globe
Organ background
Guitar accompaniment (optional)

The Message

Good morning, girls and boys! Today I want to tell you a true story about something that happened a long time ago in a place very far away.

It was in the year 1818, in a little town in Austria called Obernorf. Austria is a country on the other side of the world. See, here we are in *(your town)*, and way over here is Austria *(point to your town, and then to Austria on the globe)*.

Joseph Mohr was the assistant minister, or priest, at the Church of St. Nicholas in Obernorf. The church building was brand new, so Father Mohr was surprised as well as worried when he discovered something dreadful on December 23. It was the day before Christmas Eve. The congregation was looking forward to having Christmas Eve worship in their new church. And do you know what happened? The organ broke. It wouldn't make a sound. "What are we going to do now?" thought Father Mohr. "What is Christmas Eve service without music?"

Father Mohr thought and prayed about his problem. "Please, God," he said. "Tell me what you want me to do." Then he went out into the starry night and took a long walk. It was very late. Everyone in the village was asleep in bed. Father Mohr listened for an answer to his prayer while he walked along, but all he heard was silence. It was a silent night. (*Have organist quietly play "Silent Night" in the background, finishing at the end of the next paragraph.)*

And then it came to him. The answer to his prayer. Father Mohr went home and wrote the words to a simple, yet beautiful, Christmas song—a song that could be easily sung even without the help of an organ.

Father Mohr took the words to the church's choir director, Franz Gruber. Mr. Gruber liked the words very much. He wrote a simple, yet beautiful, melody to match the words. That Christmas Eve, the congregation of the Church of St. Nicholas sang this special carol for the very first time. With the help of a guitar, the people sang "Silent Night, Holy Night." It is, of course, one of our most favorite Christmas carols even today.

Why do you think Father Mohr was so upset when he found out the organ wouldn't play? Christmas is such a happy, joyous time! Have you ever felt so happy you could hardly stand it? It's as if your whole chest fills with joy, and you have to let it out somehow.

When Mary told her cousin, Elizabeth, that she was going to have a baby named Jesus, words were not enough. She was so thankful to God, and so full of joy about the baby, she started to sing. I think that's how Father Mohr felt about Christmas. Telling the Christmas story with words would not be enough. He knew the people in his church needed to sing their thanks and praise to God at the birth of their Savior. Singing was an important part of worship for Father Mohr and his people. Singing is an important part of our worship too.

To finish our story this morning, let's all sing "Silent Night" together. *(If possible, sing the first stanza of the carol with guitar accompaniment. Invite the congregation to join in the singing.)*

Season of Christmas

Holy Messengers

Props Needed

A Christmas card, preferably with an angel on it

The Message

Merry Christmas, everyone! I want to show you a nice Christmas card I received this past week. See, it has a pretty picture on the front, and inside there is a message. The message reads, "_____." (*Read the card.*)

My mail carrier put this card in my mailbox. You might say that he was the messenger who delivered this Christmas greeting from my friends, _____ and _____.

On the night that Jesus was born, God sent messengers with Christmas greetings. God's messengers are called angels. The angels were sent by God to deliver a special Christmas message to a group of shepherds.

Shepherds are people who take care of flocks of sheep, or sometimes goats. The shepherds were spending the night in the fields, watching their flocks. All of a sudden God's messenger, the angel, appeared to them. At first they were frightened, but the angel said to them, "Don't be afraid! Today in Bethlehem your Savior was born. You will know this is true because you will find the baby wrapped in cloths and lying in a manger."

Then the whole sky was filled with angels singing and praising God. They sang, "Glory to God in the highest heaven, and on earth peace." After they had delivered the message, the angels left.

The shepherds, of course, were amazed. They went to Bethlehem. They found Mary and Joseph in a stable. And the baby Jesus was lying in the manger, just as the angel had said.

What do you think an angel looks like? (*Give children opportunity to respond.*) We usually think of angels in long white robes, with wings, don't we? That's what the angel on this card looks like, doesn't it? (*Refer to your Christmas card if it has a "typical" angel pictured on it.*) But do you know what? Angels don't always have wings. Angels sometimes look like ordinary people. Sometimes angels look like you, or you, or you! (*Point to children.*) You may not realize this, but each one of us can be an angel.

Tell me again what an angel is. An angel is a messenger of God. We can be God's messengers by sharing the good news. Just like the angels who took God's message to the shepherds, we are God's angels whenever we share the message of Jesus' birth with others. Merry Christmas! Jesus is born! Spread the news, little angels!

Let's pray. Dear God, we thank you for the joy and love we know in Christmas. Help us to be messengers of that joy and love. May we be your angels at Christmas and all year. Amen.

Parents Are Only Human

Prop Needed

A picture of Jesus in the Temple at age twelve (often available in church school files of past curricula). If unavailable, tell the story with no prop.

The Message

Have any of you ever been lost? Have you ever been at the grocery store, or the mall, and you just stopped to look at one thing, and when you turned around, your mom or dad was gone? How does it feel to be lost and alone? (*Or* "How do you think it would feel . . . ?") How do you think your parents felt when you were lost? I'll bet they were just as frightened as you were, because they couldn't find you.

Something like this happened to Jesus and his parents when Jesus was twelve years old. They went to the big city of Jerusalem for a special holiday called the Passover. They were with a large group of people from their hometown of Nazareth.

The festival was over, and it was time to go home. It would take several days to walk from Bethlehem to Nazareth. Mary and Joseph didn't see Jesus. They assumed he was with some other members of their group, so they headed home with everyone else. In the evening Mary and Joseph set up their camp, fixed supper, and waited for Jesus to come find them. When he didn't come, they began to worry. They checked with everyone in their group, but Jesus was nowhere to be found. They returned to Jerusalem—a whole day's walk away—and looked for him there. Finally, after two days of searching, they found Jesus. Do you know where he was? (*Show picture*). He was in the Temple, learning about God. Jesus wasn't frightened. He didn't know he was lost! Jesus was surprised when his mother told him how worried they had been. He said, "Didn't you know I would be in my Father's house?" That is surely a strange thing for Jesus to say, isn't it? Jesus' house was in Nazareth, not in Jerusalem! What do you think Jesus meant when he said he was in his Father's house? *(Pause.)* He meant that he was in God's house, the house of the heavenly Father.

Mary and Joseph were relieved to find Jesus. They went home together to Nazareth, where Jesus grew up. He worked with Joseph as a carpenter until he was thirty years old, when his true work began as teacher, healer, and preacher.

We are all God's children. We all need to spend time learning about the Lord, as Jesus did. As we study about God, we learn also what God's will is for our lives—what God wants us to do and be.

Let's Pray. Dear God, thank you for caring about us so much. Help us to learn as much about you and your will for our lives as we can. Amen.

Epiphany
and the Season Following

The Very Best Christmas Present Ever

Prop Needed

A beautifully wrapped Christmas present, containing the figure of Jesus from a crèche. The gift should be marked with the tag mentioned in the story.

The Message

Good morning! Look at what I found yesterday. This unopened Christmas present! I was cleaning up some pine needles and found it shoved in a corner. Can you believe it? I guess that in all the excitement of opening gifts on Christmas morning this one was overlooked. There's a tag on it. It reads, "For anyone who wants it—The Very Best Christmas Present Ever."

This must be something really special! I wonder what it is. What do you think I should do with this present? Do you think I should open it? Really? But I'm not sure it's for me. What if it belongs to someone else? Well, the tag does say it's for anyone who wants it, doesn't it? Okay, you talked me into it. Let's open it. (*While opening the package, make comments such as, "Oh, I'm so curious! I can't imagine what this is. I could use a new pair of roller skates," etc.*)

Oh, look. We should have known. Can you tell what the very best Christmas present ever is? That's right, it's Jesus. Here, let's pass this gift around so everyone can see it.

One thing that makes this gift so special is that it's not just for one person or one group of people. The gift of Jesus is offered to anyone. God sent the gift of Jesus for you and for me—and for everybody.

Not long after Jesus was born he had some very interesting

visitors. They were not from his part of the world. They lived in a country to the east. These people noticed a new star in the sky. They followed that star until they found Jesus. And when they found him, they worshiped him. They knew that Jesus was God's gift to the world, and so they knelt down and worshiped him.

Then they gave Jesus their gifts—gold, frankincense, and myrrh. Gold was the most precious thing they had. Frankincense represented worship. And myrrh symbolized the suffering and death Jesus would go through for our sakes when he grew up. It is because these visitors brought gifts to Jesus that we give Christmas gifts to each other even today.

When someone gives you a present, what are you supposed to do? Yes, you say, "Thank you." If you know how to write, it's really nice to send a thank-you note, telling someone how much you appreciate his or her remembering you with a gift. One way we thank God for the gifts God gives us is in prayer.

Let's Pray together now. Dear, generous God, we take time now to thank you for the very best Christmas present ever. May we never shove Jesus off into a corner, but keep him at the center of our lives always. Amen.

Welcome to the Family

Prop Needed
Church's baptismal font or bowl, with water in it

The Message
I'd like you all to gather here around the baptismal font while I tell you our story this morning. (*Arrange children so they can all see the font.*)

Alyson buckled the last buckle on her patent leather shoes. She smiled her biggest smile. She ran into her baby brother's room, where their mother was getting him ready for church too.

"Look, Mommy!" Alyson said excitedly.

"Don't you look pretty!" said her mother. "And you even have your shoes on already. Did you buckle them all by yourself?" Alyson nodded. "My, what a big girl you are," her mother replied.

Alyson looked at the baby. "Mommy, why is Jimmy wearing a dress?" she asked.

"That dress is a baptismal gown, Alyson," replied her mother. "It is very special. You wore this gown when you were baptized. Your daddy and your grandpa wore it when they were baptized too."

"Tell me again what 'baptized' means," said Alyson.

" 'Baptized' means being welcomed into God's family," her mother explained. "You see, Daddy and I love God very much. God and God's church are very important to us, and we want them to be important to you and Jimmy too. And so we took you when you were a baby, and this morning we will take Jimmy to be baptized.

"During the baptism, Pastor Bob will ask Daddy and me some questions. We will tell everyone that we love God and that Jesus Christ is our Lord and Savior. We will also say that we want Jimmy to grow up loving God. We will promise to teach him about Jesus and to show him what our faith is all about. The congregation—that's all the people in the church—will promise to help us teach him too."

Just then Alyson's dad came into the room. "Everybody ready?" he asked. The four of them left for the service of worship.

When Alyson and her family arrived at the church, they found a seat near the front of the sanctuary. Everybody sang songs and said prayers. Then Alyson heard Pastor Bob say, "Will those who are to present their child for baptism please come forward?"

"That's us," whispered Alyson's dad. They scootched out the pew and walked the few steps to the front. They stood facing Pastor Bob. Next to him was a large bowl of water on a stand, like this one. Alyson remembered seeing the strange bowl before, but she never knew what it was.

Pastor Bob started talking to Alyson's parents. She didn't understand everything he said. Then he asked them the questions. Next, Pastor Bob held Jimmy in his arms. He dipped his fingers into the water and touched Jimmy's head. The water dripped down Jimmy's face, and he started to fuss. Pastor Bob rocked him back and forth while he said, "James Michael Kauffman, I baptize you in the name of the Father, and of the Son, and of the Holy Spirit. May the blessings of God, Father, Son, and Holy Spirit, be with you now and forevermore." Then Pastor Bob looked into Jimmy's smiling face and said, "Welcome to the family of God."

Let's Pray. Dear God, we thank you that we can all be members of your family. Thank you for the people who care enough about us to teach us about Jesus. May we grow in knowledge and in faith all our lives. Amen.

(You may want to invite the children to take a closer look at the font as they leave, perhaps letting them touch the water as well.)

All Kinds of Shoes

Props Needed

5 to 8 Different kinds of footwear, such as a beach sandal, bedroom slipper, rain or snow boot, athletic shoe, baby bootie, dress shoe, swim flipper. Put them in a paper sack. Adapt the story to accommodate the things in your sack.

The Message

Good morning, boys and girls! I have a lot of things in this bag that I want to show you. (*Take one out of the bag and hold it up so all the kids can see it.*)

Who can tell me what this is? Exactly right. It's something we wear on our feet. What kind is it? Right again. It's a rain boot. We wear rain boots to keep our feet dry when it's wet outside, don't we? Here's another. This one's a sandal. When do you think you might wear this sandal? Yes, to the beach or to the swimming pool. (*Continue to show footwear and discuss their functions until the sack is empty and all are lined up in front of you.*)

These are a lot of shoes, aren't they? And each has a different function, or purpose. If I were all dressed up and ready to go to a party, I wouldn't wear this one, would I? (*Hold up the bedroom slipper.*) I would look pretty silly playing tennis in something like this, right? (*Hold up the rain boot.*) And when it's nighttime, and I'm in my pajamas and robe and want to stay up just a little longer, which kind of footwear would keep my feet the warmest? Right! Slippers! So we can say that these are all footwear, but we use different kinds for different activities. Each pair of shoes or boots in our closet has a special reason for being there.

Do you know that we in the church are like this sack of

footwear? Well, we are! All of us in the church are Christians. We all love God and believe in Jesus as our Savior. We are all Christians. But we are each different, too. God has given each one of us special abilities or talents—things that we do really, really well. The Bible calls these talents spiritual gifts.

Some of us can sing or play a musical instrument. Some of us are very good at sharing. Some people in the church are great teachers, or ushers, or are good at making decisions that help run the church. Some of you may be very kind toward others, or maybe you do well in sports or math, or maybe you really know how to listen. Each one of us is extra good at something, and each of us is different.

God needs all of us in the church to use our talents to help one another. If just one person is missing, the church is not as strong or as effective as it could be. We need each person, each one of you with your own special spiritual gift, to help the church do God's work. Thank you for being here and for sharing your talents with us.

Let's Pray. Good and gracious God, we thank you for the special talents that each one of us has. May we use them in ways that make you proud of us and that help the church to be strong. Amen.

The Mystery Book

Prop Needed
A Bible

The Message

This morning I want to tell you about a very special book. This book has just about everything in it.

The book I'm thinking of contains hundreds of wonderful stories. There are stories about families and the problems they sometimes have. The father in one story liked one son best, and so his brothers sold the favorite into slavery. How they all got back together again is a fascinating tale.

There are stories about floods and earthquakes and fires. There are stories about people losing things and then finding them again. There is a story about a young boy who beats a giant and one about a woman who saves her country in a time of war. There are stories about sick people getting well. One story tells about some fishermen about to be drowned in their boat. That is an exciting one! This book contains hundreds of stories—too many for me to mention them all. It has other things in it as well.

The book I'm thinking about also has songs in it. There are beautiful love songs that one man wrote to his wife. And there are hymns like those we sing in church. Some of the hymns are happy songs of praise and thanksgiving. Other hymns sound confused or angry.

The book has prayers in it. There are letters and family records—lists of who is related to whom. It has suggestions or advice on how to live a good life. There are also some rules in this book. And even though this book was written a long, long time ago, these are still good rules for us to follow today. I think there may even be a recipe or two in this book.

Have you already guessed what book I'm describing? The most useful, interesting, exciting, important book I know is the Bible. *(Show the children your Bible.)*

I've told you all the different parts that make up the Bible— the stories, the prayers, the songs, and so on, but I haven't told you the most significant thing about it yet. What makes the Bible so truly special is that it is a book which tells us about God.

The Bible teaches us about God and about ourselves. In reading the stories and other things in the Bible, we learn that God loves us. We learn that God cares about us. When we read the Bible we also find out how God would like us to live our lives as Christians.

The Bible is not always easy to understand. I've read it over and over again, and there are still some things about it and about God that I don't get. But each time I read the Bible I learn something new, and I understand God just a little bit more. It especially helps to read the Bible with other Christians, in worship and in church school.

I know that you read the Bible here at church. I hope that you read it at home with your parents too. If you ever have any questions about something you've read, you can ask your folks, or your church school teachers, or me, and we'll all try to understand it together. You're never too young, nor too old, to read the Bible.

Let's Pray. Holy Lord God, we thank you for making yourself known to us in the Bible. Give us patience and understanding as we try to learn from it. Amen.

1 Corinthians 13:1–13

God's Special Valentine Message

Props Needed

A Valentine's Day card for your spouse, mother, or a friend—whomever you may send a valentine (Adapt the story to your circumstances.)

A piece of valentine candy, or a valentine card, for each child (optional)

The Message

I have a card that I want to show you this morning. On the front it has a picture with some hearts, a rose, and chess pieces. At the top it reads, "For My Husband." Inside is a poem, and across the bottom is written, "Happy Valentine's Day." I thought I'd sign this card and give it to Frank on Valentine's Day. I think he'll like it, because he likes to play chess. Don't tell him about it because it's a surprise, okay?

Husbands, wives, and sweethearts aren't the only people who give and receive valentines, are they? You might make a lacy valentine for your mother or your grandmother. Dads and grandpas like to receive valentines too! Valentine's Day gives us a chance to tell people close to us that we love them.

We sometimes give valentines to friends too. Children in school often take valentine cards for everyone in their class, including the teacher. How many of you take valentines for your class on Valentine's Day? Are the cards passed out sometime during the day and put in a special valentine box or bag that you have on your desk? Even if there's someone in the class whom you don't get along with very well, or whom you don't like very much, it would be very nice to bring a valentine for that person too. You wouldn't want to hurt any children's feelings by leaving them out.

Valentine's Day centers on the theme of love. The Bible centers on the theme of God's love. The Bible tells about God's love for us and the love we should have for one another.

When the Bible tells us to love each other, it doesn't mean we're supposed to go around hugging and kissing everyone we meet. Loving each other with the love of God means being kind and patient toward others. It means treating other people with respect. It means not hurting another's feelings on purpose and not always putting yourself and what you want first.

God wants us to love everyone. That is not the same as saying that we have to like everyone, or even be everyone's friend. But God does want us to treat everybody with patience, kindness, and respect. In fact, the Bible tells us that loving others with the love of God is the most important thing we can do in our lives.

Let's Pray. Great God of love, we thank you for sharing your love with us. Help us to share your love with each other. Amen.

(You may want to give each child a Valentine card or candy as they leave.)

The Greatest Fish Story

Prop Needed
A fishing pole

The Message

How many of you have ever gone fishing? (*Hold up pole.*) Did you catch any fish? If you didn't catch any fish, you probably still ate supper that night, right? You probably still had a good time fishing even if you didn't catch anything. For some people, going fishing is more than fun. It is their work, their job. If they don't catch any fish, it can be a very serious problem.

One day, many years ago, Jesus was standing on the shore of Lake Galilee. He had been preaching only a short time, but news of the new teacher who could perform miracles was spreading already. People heard that Jesus was at the lake, and many came down to the water's edge to listen to him. The crowd grew quite large and was pressing on Jesus, backing him into the water. They weren't trying to hurt Jesus. It was just that everyone wanted to be close to him at once.

Jesus spied two boats pulled up on the beach. The fishermen were through with fishing and were busy washing their nets. Jesus climbed into one of the boats. He asked Simon, who owned the boat, to push off from the shore just a little way. Jesus sat in the boat, facing the crowd on the shore, and taught them.

When he was finished talking Jesus told Simon to go to deeper water and fish again. Simon told Jesus that he and his partners had been fishing all night long and hadn't caught a single fish. Still, Simon said, "But if you say so, Master, we will let down the nets."

Simon used a great big net for fishing instead of a fishing pole. The net had weights all around its outside edge. He flung out the net (*make flinging motion with your arm*) so that it made a big circle on the water. The weights sank into the lake. Then, when the men pulled the net in this time, it was filled with tons of fish. The nets almost broke from the weight of so many fish! Simon called to his partners in the other boat for help. Both boats were so full of fish, they almost sank.

Remember, there had been no fish all night, but now with the help of Jesus both boats were overflowing with the catch. Simon realized that Jesus was a very special and very Godly man. Simon kneeled down in the boat and asked Jesus to leave. "Go away from me, Lord," he said. "I do not deserve your help. I am not good enough. I am a sinner."

Jesus said to Simon and his partners, "Do not be afraid. I need you to help me catch men and women for God." They pulled their boats back onto the shore and left them there—fish and all—and followed Jesus. They were his first disciples.

I think there is something even more amazing in this story than the enormous catch of fish. The really amazing thing is that Jesus chose ordinary people—people like the fishermen Simon, James, and John—to help him do God's work. Ordinary people are still asked to help with God's work—people like you and like me. May we be like those fishermen and follow Jesus as his disciples today.

Let's Pray. Dear God, help us to follow Jesus and to be his disciples as did Simon, James, and John. Be with us as we continue to do God's work in the world. Amen.

Bitter Sweets

Prop Needed
A candy bar

The Message
Maggie sat at her desk, trying to remember what twelve times twelve equaled. Jennifer Jump raised her hand. "One hundred forty-four," she said. "Very good, Jenny," said Ms. Karnop. "You may write the answer on the chalkboard."

"Shoot!" thought Maggie. Her third-grade class had been working on the multiplication tables all year, and she still didn't know the twelves very well. Even though she and Jenny were best friends, Maggie wished she could be the one writing "144" on the board.

"Brrring!" the bell sounded. "Class dismissed," said Ms. Karnop. Maggie put her social studies book, her math book, and her copy of *Charlotte's Web* in her backpack. "Ready to go?" Maggie looked up to find Jenny, Katie, and Alyson. "Sure," Maggie said to her friends. The four girls started walking home together.

"I'm starved. Want to stop by Mr. Samford's store on the way home?" Jenny asked. Katie and Alyson nodded yes. Maggie said, "But I don't have any money." "Oh, that's okay," Jenny said. "You can just come in with us."

Mr. Samford's store wasn't very large, but one entire aisle was devoted to candy. The girls walked up and down the aisle several times, trying to decide which kind they wanted. Maggie kept staring at the bright-colored wrapper of her favorite bar. (*Hold up the candy bar.*) Her stomach growled. "Why don't you just take it?" Jenny asked. "I can't do that!" answered Maggie. "I don't want to get into trouble." "Who's going to know?" asked Jenny. "Besides, look at all this candy! Mr. Samford isn't going to miss one little candy bar. Go ahead, while no one's looking."

Maggie didn't move. "What's the matter? You chicken?" That did it. No one called Maggie Morgan chicken! She grabbed the candy and shoved it into her pocket. "I'll wait for you outside," she told Jenny and ran out the door.

Jenny, Katie, and Alyson ate their candy bars while they laughed and talked the rest of the way home. Maggie ate her candy bar in silence. For some reason, it didn't taste as good as usual.

When Maggie got to her house, her mom was working in the yard. "Hi, Mags! How was school today?" she asked. "Okay," Maggie said quietly. "What is that all over your face? Is it dirt?" asked her mother. "Bye, Maggie! See you tomorrow!" said her friends as they walked on down the street.

Maggie turned to her mom. "No, it's not dirt on my face," she said. "What is it then?" "It's chocolate," replied Maggie. "Oh, Mom, I didn't mean to steal it, honest I didn't, but Jenny called me 'chicken' and . . ." Maggie started to cry. Her mother held her in her arms and then listened to the whole story. Finally Maggie said, "I'm really, really sorry."

Maggie's mother then said, "I'm glad to hear you say you're sorry, Maggie. Taking things that don't belong to you is very, very wrong. It's against the laws of our country, and it's also against God's law. So when you steal something, you not only disappoint me and others who care about you, you also disappoint God. And I think you disappointed yourself too, didn't you? You must never let your friends talk you into doing something that you know in your heart is wrong. Well, you already ate the candy, so we can't return it, but I think I know a way you can make things right."

Maggie and her mother went back to Mr. Samford's store. Maggie told Mr. Samford what she had done. She paid for the candy bar out of her own money, told Mr. Samford how sorry she was, and offered to sweep the floor of his store for him. "Thank you, Maggie, I would appreciate that," Mr. Samford said. When she was finished, Maggie and her mom went home together.

Let's Pray. Dear God, help us to do the right thing. We want you to be proud of us. Amen.

Do Unto Others . . .

Prop Needed
A child's toy

The Message

Good morning. Today we're going to talk about Jesus. We hear a lot about Jesus in church. That's because one of the reasons we come to church is to learn about Jesus. We in the church believe that Jesus was, and is, a very special person.

Jesus was a preacher who changed many people's lives with his wise sermons. He was a healer who could make sick people feel well again. And he was a teacher whose followers learned from what he said and from how he lived his life.

Some people would walk for miles and miles to hear Jesus speak, because they liked what he was teaching them. Other people became very angry when they heard Jesus' lessons and wanted him to stop teaching.

Jesus did have some pretty crazy ideas. For example, let's say I give this toy to Jimmy here to play with. (*Give one child the toy, using his or her name, if possible.*) Now imagine that Kathryn over there grabs it away from Jimmy. Jimmy would probably shout something like, "Hey, wait a minute! I had it first! You have to wait your turn!" Who would be right? (*Wait for answers.*) Jimmy would be right, of course! Because according to the rules of childhood, the one who has something first gets to play with it until it's the next person's turn, right?

Do you know what Jesus would say? Jimmy should let Kathryn have the first turn even though he had the toy first. Jesus also taught that when someone is mean to us, we should be nice to them. And we need to love our enemies instead of hate them. Love our enemies! Sounds pretty crazy, doesn't it?

But maybe these aren't such crazy ideas after all. Basically, Jesus was saying that we should treat other people the way we would like to be treated ourselves. Can you imagine what the world would be like if everyone followed Jesus' teachings? If everyone were sharing, and kind, and loving? I think the world would be a much better place, don't you?

A good place to start making the world better is right here, with ourselves. Let's all try to treat other people the way we would like to be treated.

Let's Pray. Dear God, Jesus' teachings sound crazy in a world where selfishness motivates so many of our actions. Help us to be crazy enough to think of others first and to treat them with kindness and love. In Jesus' name we pray. Amen.

Rock-Solid Faith

Props and Preparation Needed
Two 9″ × 13″ baking pans
Sand
1 Large stone
1 Pitcher of water
Pile the sand in one baking dish so that it looks like a small hill. In the other baking dish, place the stone.
1 Small stone for each child (optional)

The Message
How many of you have heard the word "faith"? Faith is kind of a hard word to explain. It can mean several things at once.

We can have faith in other people. Your parents may say, "I have faith in you," as they're leaving you with a sitter or on your own for the first time. That means they trust you to be good while they're away.

We also talk about the Christian faith. Our religious faith has to do with what we believe and with how we live. The Bible tells us again and again that if we say we believe in God, yet treat other people badly, we are lying. If we truly believe in God, then we will try our best to be the kind of people God wants us to be. What does God expect from people of the Christian faith? Does God want us to be honest? To be caring? What else? (*Pause for answers.*) We call obedience to God "practicing our faith." So faith involves what we believe and what we do.

Jesus explained faith this way. (*Place the props in position so all can see.*) He said that anyone who believes in him and obeys his teachings to love one another is like this: That person's faith is as solid as a rock. (*Point to the stone in the pan.*) And suppose that person comes upon hard, stormy times in life. (*Pour water over stone.*) The solid rock of his or her faith will provide strong support when needed until the stormy troubles pass and things get better.

But what about those who say they believe yet ignore Jesus' teachings to love one another? Their faith is as slippery as sand. (*Point to pan with the sand.*) When stormy times of trouble come to them (*pour water over sand*), they cannot depend on their faith to help them. They just slosh around in the muck, wondering whatever went wrong, because they never had true faith in the first place.

Strong, dependable faith is based on the solid rock of firm belief and on obedience to God. We need to practice our faith to make it strong.

Let's Pray. Almighty and Everlasting God, please help us to practice what we believe. Help us to be the kind of people you want us to be. And when we fail, forgive us. Amen.

(*You may want to give each child a small stone as they leave.*)

Get Your Clothes Dazzling Bright

Prop Needed

A box or bottle of laundry detergent

The Message

Have any of you ever gone to the grocery store and noticed all the different kinds of laundry detergents there are on the shelves? There are liquid detergents and powdered detergents. Some come in bottles, some come in boxes. The packages are all brightly colored, each one made to look more interesting than the next so that you will buy it instead of another brand. On the TV commercials the manufacturers each claim that their soap makes clothes cleaner and brighter than anybody else's, don't they? This is the laundry detergent I bought this week. (*Show prop.*)

Some people have their favorite kinds of soap. What kind does your family use? (*Pause for answers.*) I think that one kind is probably just as good as the next. I bought this brand because I had a dollar-off coupon for it.

The story I want to tell you today isn't really about laundry soap. But it does have dazzling white clothes in it. The story took place soon after Jesus' disciples realized how special Jesus was. They realized that Jesus was sent by God to forgive all people of their sin. Jesus knew that being God's Chosen One would not be easy. He knew that some people would listen to what he had to say and follow his teachings. Jesus also knew that other people would be jealous of him and try to hurt him. For Jesus, obeying God was not an easy thing. Jesus knew that obeying God might get him into a lot of trouble with those who didn't like what he taught. As you can imagine, Jesus needed extra strength from God to face what was ahead of him. And so Jesus took three of his best friends, Peter, James, and John, and they went up on a hill to pray.

Jesus must have been praying a long time, because his friends fell asleep. When they woke up they could hardly believe their eyes. Jesus' face looked different. It had a special glow to it, and his clothes were dazzling bright! The Bible says they were brighter than anyone in the world could wash them. It wouldn't matter which laundry detergent they used! Standing next to Jesus were the ancient prophet Elijah and Moses. They told Jesus that he would soon save God's people by dying in Jerusalem.

The disciples didn't understand what was happening. Then they heard God say, "This is my Son . . . Listen to him!" Moses and Elijah disappeared, and Jesus looked normal again.

God gave Jesus the strength he needed to obey God, no matter how hard it was. Jesus' shining face and dazzling clothes were a touch of heaven and a promise of the future, just when Jesus and his friends needed it most.

We may not face the same kind of problems Jesus did, but God promises to give us strength when we have tough times too. God's promise to Jesus is God's promise to us, because Jesus did obey God and died for our sins.

Let's Pray. Dear God, we thank you for giving Jesus and the disciples the hope and strength they needed so that we might inherit the promise of eternal life. In the name of Jesus the Christ, we pray. Amen.

Season of Lent

Lenten Surprises

Props and Preparation Needed

1 Paper lunch sack
1 Purple sheet with the word "LENT" printed on it
40 Jelly beans
1 Glass bowl
Put the purple sheet and the jelly beans in the sack.

The Message

Hi, everyone! Can anyone guess what might be in this paper sack? Let me give you a hint. (*Shake the sack.*) There are a lot of different things that could be in here, aren't there? Why don't we just look inside and find out what it is. (*Open the sack. First remove the banner, unroll it, and hold it up so the children can all see it.*)

There is a paper banner with the letters L-E-N-T on it. Does anyone know what L-E-N-T spells? It Spells "Lent." (*Put banner where all can see it.*)

That's a pretty banner, but I'm sure that's not what was making all the noise when we shook the sack. There must be something else in here. (*Look inside.*) Ah, there is! Would you please hold this for me? (*Have a child hold the glass bowl while you pour in the jelly beans.*) Jelly beans! That is a lot of jelly beans. Let's count them and see exactly how many there are. (Count them one by one back into the sack, then pour them into the bowl again.)

A purple banner with the word "Lent" on it and forty jelly beans. These things tell us something about why today is a special day for Christians.

Today is the first Sunday of the season called Lent. You know the calendar year is divided into four seasons. Can you remember what they are? Yes—winter, spring, summer, and fall. The church divides the year into seasons too, only church seasons remind us of things that happened in Jesus' life.

The Season of Lent is the forty days before Easter. That's why we have forty jelly beans—forty candies for forty days, and jelly beans for Easter! Easter is the day of Jesus' resurrection. We will talk more about that in a few weeks. Each church season has its own special color. The color for Lent is purple, just like the color of our banner.

Lent is a time when Christians everywhere prepare themselves for Easter. In some countries, people scrub their homes from top to bottom. Some of us buy new clothes for Easter or make special foods. We color eggs, don't we? But I'm not really talking about that kind of preparation. During Lent we try extra hard to get ready for Easter on the inside. We think about how we might be better people. How can we be better Christians? When during the past year did we disappoint God? Maybe at some time we didn't tell the truth, or disobeyed our parents or teacher. Maybe we didn't help someone when we could have, or were mean to our brothers or sisters. Lent gives us a special time to tell God we're sorry and that we will try to do better.

Do you know the really great part? God hears us. When we do something wrong and tell God we're sorry, the Lord hears us, listens to us, and forgives us. Not only that, but God is our friend and helps us try to do better next time. Telling God we're sorry and trying to do better helps us get ready for the miracle of Jesus' resurrection at Easter. And that is what Lent is all about.

Let's Pray. Our dear friend God, we thank you for this special season called Lent. Thank you for helping us to be the best people we can be. In Jesus' name we pray. Amen.

(You may want to give the children each a jelly bean as they leave.)

God Keeps Promises

Prop Needed

A family heirloom (An antique toy would be perfect, but anything passed down one or two generations would work. A member of the congregation might be recruited to show his or her heirloom to the children. The message will need to be adapted depending on the particular object.)

The Message

Storyteller: Good morning, boys and girls! Do all of you know Mr. Jones, from our church? Mr. Jones is here to share something very special with us.

Mr. Jones: Hello, children! Can anyone guess what this is? (*Hold up object.*) Yes, it is a toy. It is an old-fashioned piggy bank. Let me show you how it works. (*Demonstrate toy, if mechanical.*) This bank is very old. It used to belong to my grandfather. He gave it to his daughter, my mother, who gave it to me. And someday I will give this bank to one of my children.

Storyteller: Thank you, Mr. Jones. Our story this morning is about someone who lived a long, long time ago. His name was Abraham. Abraham had something special that he gave to his children. Then they passed it down to their children, kind of like the way Mr. Jones's family passed the bank from one generation to the next. Only the something special Abraham had wasn't a toy. It wasn't an object you could hold in your hand. What Abraham passed on to his children was a promise—a promise that God had given to him.

God promised Abraham three things. God promised many descendants—lots of children and grandchildren and great-grandchildren. God also promised Abraham a land that would be their own. Abraham was what we call a nomad. He lived in a tent and moved around all the time, so he really didn't have a home.

The third thing God promised was the most precious of all. It was more important than a big family, more important than a home. God promised to love and care for Abraham and Sarah and their children. It meant that God would help them when they were in trouble and be their friend all the time. Abraham's family would be the family of God.

God's promise to Abraham was passed down through the ages and is still God's promise to us today. And just as God kept the promise to Abraham, God keeps the same promise to us.

Let's Pray. God, who keeps promises, we are glad to be part of your family. Thank you for being dependable. We know you will always keep your promises to us, and that helps us to feel safe. We know you will always love us, and we love you too. Amen.

A Direct Line to Heaven

Prop Needed
A toy telephone

The Message

You all know what this is, don't you? (*Hold up toy phone.*) Sure, it's a toy telephone. This one makes a ringing sound when you turn the dial, and then you can answer it. (*Pretend to answer the phone.*) Hello? Yes, she's here. Just a minute. (*Hold the receiver up to a child nearby and say,*) "It's for you." Many small children learn how to talk on a real telephone by practicing on a toy phone like this one. How many of you answer the phone when it rings at your house? What do you say when you answer the phone?

Moses was a man who received a call from God. God didn't call Moses on a telephone, but Moses heard the Lord loud and clear.

The Bible tells us that Moses was taking care of a flock of sheep and goats on a mountain called Mount Sinai. Moses was walking along with the animals when he spotted something strange in the distance. It looked as though a bush were on fire. But there was something different about it. Moses went closer and saw that there were flames, but the leaves and the wood on the bush were not burning up! The leaves were still green, and the bark was still fresh. Moses took a step closer and heard a voice come out of the bush.

"Moses! Moses!" the voice said.

Moses answered, "Yes, here I am."

"Do not come any closer. Take off your sandals, because you are standing on holy ground. I am the Lord."

It was God talking to Moses out of that burning bush. Why do you suppose God was talking to Moses? There was a job God needed to have done, and Moses was the person chosen to do it.

God's people, the Hebrews, were slaves in a country called Egypt. They were being treated unfairly, and they prayed to God for help. God wanted Moses to go to Egypt, help the Hebrews escape, and lead them into freedom. God wanted Moses to take the people to the land that God had promised Abraham so many years before.

Moses heard what God wanted him to do loud and clear. But he wasn't sure he could do it. He came up with a whole list of reasons why he couldn't do the job. But each time he thought of an excuse, God found a solution to Moses' problem. Finally, God simply told him to stop worrying. God was not going to send Moses to Egypt alone. The Lord would be with him, telling him what to do and what to say.

Moses said yes, with God's help, he would lead the people out of Egypt. God helped Moses, and Moses helped God to save the Hebrew people from slavery and lead them safely into the Promised Land.

Sometimes we are asked to do things that may seem too hard for us, just as Moses was. But if we ask, there is usually someone who can help us. It may be someone in our family, a teacher at school, or a friend from church. And along with these folks, God is always with us. God is always ready to help us, giving us courage and strength.

Let's Pray. God, you are always with us, helping us, making us strong, showing us the way to go. Let us agree to help others, even if the job seems too hard, because we know you are with us. In Jesus' name we pray. Amen.

Love That Cannot Be Broken

Prop Needed
A broken object (adapt story to fit your object)

The Message
Can everyone see what I have with me this morning? Can you tell me what it was before it was broken? It used to be a teacup. I want to tell you a story about a broken teacup and two children who learned an important lesson about love from it.

Once there was a woman named Mrs. Miller, who owned a beautiful teacup. It was fragile and delicate and had pretty blue flowers painted on it. It was her favorite teacup. She kept it sitting on a shelf way up high in her living room. Sometimes Mrs. Miller would take it down and drink her tea out of it. Then she would carefully wash and dry it and put it back in its place on the high shelf.

Mrs. Miller had two children named Ben and Kristina. They had their own bedrooms, with lots of nice toys in them. Sometimes they played in their bedrooms. They were also allowed to play in the kitchen, the cellar, and the back yard. In fact, there was only one place in the whole house where they were not supposed to play—the living room.

One day Ben and Kristina were on their way to the back yard to play catch. They started tossing the ball back and forth as they walked through the house. In the living room, Ben threw a high fly to Kristina. She jumped to catch the ball, but missed. The ball hit the shelf where their mother's favorite teacup was sitting and sent it crashing to the floor. The two children looked at each other. They felt terrible. What was their mother going to do to them? They left the mess on the floor and ran outside. They decided to hide in the garage for a year or so, until their mother stopped being angry at them.

A few minutes went by. They heard their mom calling them from the back porch. Her voice sounded angry, all right. They were quiet, and their mom went back inside the house. About five minutes passed, and they heard their names called again, "Ben! Kristina!" This time their mother's voice seemed softer. They could hear her walk around the side of the house, calling their names. "Ben! Kristina!" She sounded closer, and they realized she was heading toward the garage! She opened the door and sunlight streamed in. They tried to make themselves smaller so she couldn't see them, but she walked right to where they were huddled.

Do you know what she did then? She put her arms around both of her children and gave them a big squeeze. "I am so glad I found you," she said. "You two had me terribly worried!"

Ben and Kristina told their mother they were afraid because they had accidentally broken her teacup, and they didn't know what she would do. They were afraid that maybe she wouldn't love them anymore.

Their mother smiled sort of a sad smile and said, "My dear Ben and Kristy. I must tell you I was not happy when I found my teacup broken on the floor. But don't you know that you two children are more important to me than anything in the world? I may not always like what you do, like playing catch in the living room, but I will always love you. No matter what."

With that, Kristy and Ben gave their mom a big hug and a kiss. They apologized for breaking the cup and promised never to play in the living room again. Then they all went inside the house to clean up the mess.

Kristina and Ben learned an important lesson that day. Sometimes we all do things that make our parents angry. They may not like what we do, but our parents still love us. The same thing is true of God. God doesn't always like what we do, but God will never stop loving us. God loves you just because you're you, even when you make a mistake.

Let's Pray. All-loving God, it is so wonderful to know that you love us just the way we are. Thank you for giving us parents to care for us.

One Great God, One Great Hour

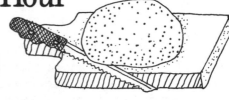

Props Needed

1 Loaf of unsliced bread (or more, depending on the size of your group)

A bread knife

A cutting board

Napkins

OGHS banks

The Message

Have all of you received your banks for One Great Hour of Sharing? (*Hold up bank. Distribute banks to any who don't have one.*) Are you remembering to fill up your banks at home? I'm glad, because the money we give to One Great Hour of Sharing helps many people in many different ways. I want to tell you about just one way our offering helps people.

Pretend that you didn't have breakfast this morning. Now pretend that you didn't have anything to eat for supper last night. Make believe that for lunch yesterday all you had was a little bowl of rice with a few vegetables in it. And you didn't have any breakfast yesterday, either. How do you feel? HUNGRY! Really, really hungry, right?

I am surely sorry you are so hungry. Is there anything I can do to help you? Oh, I know! I have this nice loaf of bread here. Let me share my bread with you. (*Cut the bread into as many slices as there are children and give each child a piece.*) You may eat that now if you'd like. You haven't eaten in a long time! Feel better? Good. Now, what happens if you don't have any more food today? What will happen tomorrow? You will be hungry again, won't you?

It helped a little bit when I shared my bread with you. It stopped your hunger right now. But what you really need is a way to stop your hunger forever, isn't it? This is what some of our One Great Hour of Sharing money does. It helps to stop people's hunger forever.

OGHS gives people food when they're hungry. At the same time, it gives them seeds and tools and fertilizer and knowledge, so that they can grow their own food. Once their crops grow, people can feed themselves and their families and maybe even help others who are hungry.

Helping others is a way of helping God and thanking God for all that we have been given. Putting money into our OGHS banks and bringing them to church on Palm Sunday (or whenever your collection date is), is a good way to help others.

Let's Pray. Good and generous God, you have given us so much— people to love us, food to eat, a place to live, a church to belong to, a life to enjoy. We want to thank you by helping others. Please use our money to feed hungry people and to help them grow their own food. Amen.

Luke 19:28–40

"Hosanna, Hurray!"

Props Needed
A palm branch for each child (may be ordered from a florist)
A picture of a palm tree (optional)

The Message
Does anyone know what special day this is? This is Palm Sunday. What is a palm? A palm is part of a certain kind of tree. It is the branch of a palm tree. I have a palm branch for each one of you. (*Pass out palms.*) I am going to ask you to help me with the story later, using your palms. But for right now, I'd like you to please hold them still on your laps.

There were lots of palm trees in Jerusalem, the city where our story takes place. (*If you live in an area where palm trees are scarce, show the picture of the palm tree. Point out the trunk and the palms.*)

Jesus was getting ready to go to Jerusalem. Usually when we go on a trip somewhere, we are pretty excited about it, aren't we? Jesus was not looking forward to going on his trip to Jerusalem, though. There were a lot of important leaders in the city who were angry with Jesus. These leaders were called scribes and Pharisees. The scribes and Pharisees didn't understand the miracles Jesus performed, and they didn't like the lessons he taught. They were afraid that the people would like Jesus more than they liked them. And so it was really dangerous for Jesus to go back to Jerusalem. But he felt that God wanted him there, and so he went.

Jesus had his disciples get a donkey for him to ride into the city. Jerusalem had a wall going all around it. In the wall were gates, where the people went in and out. Jesus rode through a gate on the back of a donkey.

Jerusalem was a very crowded city. There were always a lot of people there. When Jesus rode through the gate, many people recognized him. He was the man who performed miracles and taught about God's love. The great crowd of people became very excited. They started shouting, "God bless the king who comes in the name of the Lord! Hosanna!" Some people laid their coats on the road in front of Jesus' donkey. Others tore palm branches off the trees and waved them as they shouted, "Hosanna!" "Hosanna" means "Yea, God!" Can you pretend that you are the people in the crowd in Jerusalem? Wave your palm branches and shout, "Yea, God! Hosanna! Hosanna!" Oh, you can be a little louder than that! "Hosanna!"

The greeting the people gave Jesus that day was the same kind of greeting they would give a king who was visiting the city. When a king came to Jerusalem, the people would put their coats and palm branches on the ground where the king's horse walked. And they would shout greetings of welcome and praise to him.

The people had heard about all the marvelous things Jesus had done. Some of them felt that Jesus should be their leader instead of the ones they already had. That was exactly what the scribes and the Pharisees were afraid of. They did not like Jesus' being welcomed into Jerusalem as if he were a king. They got together and planned ways to make trouble for Jesus. But on Palm Sunday, most of the people were overjoyed that Jesus had come to Jerusalem. "Hosanna! Hurray, God!"

Let's Pray. Great and glorious God, we give you thanks and praise for your goodness. May we worship you with our voices, with our hearts, and with our lives. Amen.

Season of Easter

Luke 24:1–12

Empty Tomb, Full of Promise

Props Needed

1 Empty Easter egg (may be plain or fancy, ceramic, papier mâché, or plastic)

1 Empty plastic egg for each child

The Message

I have something with me that I think you'll recognize. (*Show the Easter egg.*) It's an Easter egg, isn't it? What do you think might be in this Easter egg? (*Allow children to guess.*) It could be filled with jelly beans or chocolate eggs. Or maybe there's a toy bunny in it. Let's open it and see, okay? Well, look at that! What's in it? Nothing! It's empty! Are you surprised to find the egg empty?

Easter is a special day full of surprises. Did you find some surprises at your house this morning? Well, the biggest Easter surprise of all was not given by the Easter Bunny, it was given by God. And God did not leave the biggest Easter surprise in a basket, but in a tomb.

Last week we talked about Jesus riding into Jerusalem on Palm Sunday. The people treated him like a king. But I told you that not everyone was thrilled to see Jesus. The religious leaders did not like Jesus, and so they plotted against him. By the end of the week, it looked as if Jesus' enemies had won. On Friday, Jesus was killed. Instead of being treated like a king, he was hung on a cross like a criminal. His friends put his body into a grave called a tomb. It was like a cave with a stone shelf in it, where they laid Jesus.

Three days later it was Sunday again. Some women who were

friends of Jesus went to the tomb. They expected to see Jesus' body. When they stepped inside the tomb they were surprised, because they didn't find a body at all. The tomb was empty, just like this Easter egg!

Jesus's friends were not only surprised; they were confused too. Suddenly two men appeared to them. They said something even more surprising, "Why are you looking among the dead for one who is alive? He is not here; he has been raised."

Jesus was not dead after all! God had raised Jesus to new life. Jesus' enemies did not win. Even though they put him to death, God raised Jesus back to life. We call that resurrection. Ressurection is the greatest surprise and the greatest gift God has ever given the world. Jesus' resurrection is what we celebrate each Easter.

I want to give each of you an Easter egg this morning. Each time you see this empty egg, remember that the greatest Easter surprise is an empty tomb and resurrection.

Let's Pray. Great God, we are not always ready for the wonderful surprises you have for us. We thank you for the empty tomb, Easter morning, and the life of hope we live because of the resurrection. In Jesus' name we pray. Amen.

Doubting Thomas

Props Needed
Flannel board
Flannel-board figures (found in the Appendix)

The Message
Our story for this morning begins the evening of the day Jesus was resurrected. You remember what happened. Some women who were friends of Jesus had gone to his tomb early in the morning and had found it empty. They were told that Jesus was no longer dead. He was raised to new life.

That must have been a pretty hard story to believe, don't you think? Of course, all of Jesus' friends and followers would want it to be true, but how could it be? When the women told the disciples what they had seen and heard, they couldn't quite believe it at first. Resurrection? It seemed impossible.

So it's really not surprising that in the evening most of Jesus' close followers were gathered together. They weren't having a party to celebrate the resurrection. They were hiding out, confused and afraid. (*Begin to follow the story with flannel-board figures. Put up apartment outlines, the disciples, and the women.*)

All of a sudden Jesus stood in the room with them. "Peace be with you," he said. He showed them the hurt places on his hands and feet, and finally Jesus' disciples and friends were able to believe. They were filled with joy. Jesus blessed them with the Holy Spirit and then left.

One disciple was not there when Jesus appeared. His name was Thomas. When Thomas came back to the house where the others were, they told him what had happened. Still Thomas would not believe. "I must see Jesus for myself," he said.

A week later the disciples were all together again, including Thomas. Once more Jesus appeared to them. "Peace be with you," he said. This time, even Thomas believed Jesus was alive. He said, "My Lord and my God."

Jesus responded to Thomas in a very interesting way. He wasn't angry. He knew the resurrection was a pretty incredible miracle. Not all people were going to believe right away, not even all of Jesus' friends. But Jesus was a little disappointed. He said, "Do you believe because you see me? How happy are those who believe without seeing me."

Whom do you suppose Jesus was talking about? Who are the people who believe even though they haven't seen Jesus? We are! All the Christians who have lived since the time of Christ are those who believe even though we haven't seen Jesus with our eyes. We believe because we see with our hearts and know that the resurrection is the truth. We are Easter people! Jesus said we would be blessed for our faith, and so we are.

We also know that if we have questions or doubts about our faith, it's okay. God will understand. Don't be afraid to ask questions. We are all here to help each other understand God and grow in faith together.

Let's Pray. Great miracle-making God, we thank you for the gift of faith. Thank you for making us Easter people. Help us to ask questions and share doubts we may have, because this is the way we learn and grow. In the name of Jesus, our risen Lord, we pray. Amen.

Feed My Lambs

Prop Needed

A dog or cat dish (You may tailor the opening of the story to accommodate your particular pet. If you have no pet, omit the personal references. You may want to use a live pet for your prop instead of the dish.)

The Message

Today I have a dog dish with me. This dish belongs to my dog, Ralph. Every day Ralph eats his food out of this bowl. Do any of you have a pet? What kinds of pets do you have? (*Allow children to answer.*) Do you help take care of your pets?

Caring for a pet can be a lot of work. You have to make sure it has plenty of food and water. You sometimes have to clean up after pets; for instance, you may have to clean a bird or hamster cage, a fish bowl, or a litter box. Some pets need to be bathed and brushed or taken for walks. Some pets need to be trained. When they get sick, pets need to be taken to the vet. When you go away, you need to find someone to look after your pet. And all pets need attention—petting or cuddling or being talked to.

Yes, pets can be a lot of work, all right. Why do you think people bother with them? Besides being a lot of work, sometimes pets are quite expensive to take care of, too. Why do some of you go to so much trouble to take care of your pets? (*Some possible answers may be "Because he needs me" or "She'd get sick or starve if I didn't take care of her." Pick up on "Because we love them."*) We take care of our pets because we love them, don't we? When you love something or someone, you want to take care of him or her.

Jesus had a disciple named Peter. One day, after his resurrection, Jesus appeared to the disciples while they were fishing. Jesus asked, "Peter, do you love me?" Peter answered, "Yes, Lord. You know I love you." Then Jesus said to Peter, "Feed my lambs."

What Jesus, the Good Shepherd, meant was, "Take care of my people." If Peter truly loved Jesus, then it was his responsibility and privilege to care for those whom Jesus loved.

The same is true today. Jesus asks those who love him to care for others. That is why we always try to be kind to our neighbors and to share with our playmates—because Jesus asked us to take care of his people.

It is also why the church builds hospitals, schools, and churches around the world. We build hospitals to take care of people's bodies—their physical health. We also help build clean water systems and develop better farming techniques for those who need them, so that God's people can have strong bodies. We build schools so children and young people can learn and develop strong minds. And we build churches so that people can have a strong, healthy faith. When we care for others, we show Jesus that we love him, and we grow to love our neighbors around the world as he does.

Let's Pray. Dear God, we celebrate the resurrection with loving acts toward other people. May your name be praised in all we do. In the name of our risen Christ we pray. Amen.

Flower Power

Props Needed
1 Daffodil bulb
1 Daffodil bloom

The Message
Can anyone tell me what this is? *(Hold up the daffodil bulb.)* It is kind of an ugly-looking thing, isn't it—all brown and lumpy. It looks like something dead, doesn't it? Well, it is a daffodil bulb. Believe it or not, from this rather ugly, dead-looking thing come beautiful flowers like this. *(Show the blooming stem.)*

This is how it works. You plant the bulb in the fall—September or October. It stays in the ground all winter long and seems to do nothing. But in the spring little green nubs first poke through the soil. These nubs grow into tall, slender leaves. The bulb also sends up a long stem with a tight bud on the end of it. The bud bursts into a fantastic flower, like this one.

There is a story about an elderly lady who had a large spot behind her garage where she grew daffodils.* One September the lady sold her house, and a family with two teenage children moved in. They liked to play basketball, so they helped their dad pave over the space behind the garage with asphalt for a basketball court.

The kids played in their heavy coats when there wasn't any snow on the court that winter. But as the weather got warmer, they noticed something strange—something amazing. The asphalt was getting bumpy. Then it cracked and began to fall

*Based on an anecdote published in *The Pastor's Story File* newsletter.

apart. In the cracks, little green nubs could be seen. The daffodil plants had pushed themselves up, through that asphalt barrier, into the spring sunshine. Those were powerful flowers!

The story of the daffodils reminds me of the Easter story. Jesus died and was buried in the tomb, just as the daffodil bulbs were buried in the ground under the asphalt. Three days later something amazing happened. The power of God broke through the barrier of death and raised Jesus to new life. Asphalt could not hold down those daffodils. Death could not hold down Jesus.

The news of new life for Jesus means new life for all who believe in him. This is the best news the world has ever received. New life for Jesus and for those who follow him is called good news, or the good news of the gospel. God wants everyone to know that Jesus has been raised to new life and that all people are invited to share in that miracle. The most important job the church has is to spread the good news throughout the world.

Let's Pray. Dear God, we thank you for the miracle of resurrection. We thank you for the gift of new life. Help us to spread the good news. Amen.

A New, Improved
Commandment

Prop Needed

A product, such as laundry soap or breakfast cereal, with the words "New! Improved!" on it. Adapt the story's opening to suit your product.

The Message

Good morning, girls and boys! I am so excited today. I was in the grocery store yesterday, and look what I found. (*Show your prop.*) Corn flakes! These aren't just any old corn flakes, though. These are new and improved! Someone at the corn flakes company must have come up with a recipe, or a way of cooking it, that would make the cereal taste better than before. I've always liked corn flakes, but I bet I'll *love* these!

Companies that make things often come up with a new, improved version of what they're selling. Jesus told his disciples that he had a new, improved commandment that he wanted them to follow. Do you know what a commandment is? It is a rule, or a law. Countries, states, and cities have laws their citizens are expected to obey. What are some laws we follow every day? (*Pause for answers. You may need to help get children started: Do not steal, do not hit other people, wait for the "Walk" signal when crossing a busy street, etc.*)

Religions also have rules, or laws, to obey. When God give a law, it's often called a commandment. God's most famous laws are called the Ten Commandments. Can you remember what any of the Ten Commandments are? (*Pause for answers, then fill in where necessary.*)

1. Worship no god but the Lord.
2. Do not worship idols or things.

3. Do not curse.
4. Rest and worship God on the Sabbath.
5. Respect your mother and father.
6. Do not murder, or kill, anyone.
7. Love the person you're married to in a special way.
8. Do not steal.
9. Do not blame a person for something he or she didn't do.
10. Do not wish for things other people have.

Those are the Ten Commandments. The people of God were expected to follow hundreds of other laws, too—laws about how and what to eat, how to treat one another in business, how to worship. There was a lot to remember!

Finally, Jesus said, "Wait a minute! I have a new commandment to give you: Love one another. Love one another the same way that I have loved you."

The interesting thing is that if you obey Jesus' new commandment to love one another, you'll be following the old law as well. If you love someone, you aren't going to rob or murder or try to hurt that person in any way. But Jesus' new commandment is a lot easier to remember: Love one another.

Let's Pray. Dear God, help us to love one another as Jesus loves us. Amen.

The Invisible Friend

Prop Needed
None

The Message

Hi, everybody! This morning I want you to meet someone. His name is Maximillian Cornelius Pendergast III. But you can call him Max. Max, these are my friends. Friends, this is Max. (*Point to the air next to you.*)

Say "Hi" to the kids, Max. What? You don't want to? Well, that's kind of rude. (*To the kids:*) Max may have a fancy name, but he is really very shy. Oh, and you may have noticed one other unusual thing about Max. He's invisible.

Do any of you have invisible friends? Or do you remember having invisible friends when you were younger? What's that, Max? Max said that some of his best friends are invisible.

Invisible friends can be rather handy to have around. With invisible friends, you always have someone to talk to and share your troubles with, even when everyone else is too busy to listen. They can be good company when you're lonely. Invisible friends can help chase monsters and other scary things out of dark corners so that you're not so afraid at night. Invisible friends are there whenever you need them, night or day. Sometimes invisible friends even take the blame when you do something wrong, such as spilling a glass of milk or splashing too much water out of the bathtub.

In many ways, Jesus is like an invisible friend. Jesus is with us always. We can't see him or touch him, but we know he is here. You can talk with Jesus and share your troubles with him. Jesus helps us to face the scary things in life. He often told his disciples, "Do not be afraid. I am with you always." He gives us the same message. "Do not be afraid. I am with you always."

And Jesus took the blame for all the wrongs we do, all the mistakes we make. He died on the cross to forgive our sins and to give us eternal life through him.

There are some ways in which Jesus and invisible friends are different too. As children get older, they usually give up their invisible friends. They outgrow their need for them, just as you outgrew last summer's sneakers. Bigger kids find other play-mates, other friends, other activities to keep their interest. But we never outgrow our need for Jesus. Jesus is our friend all our life. Young people, old people, and people in between all depend on Jesus for friendship and help and salvation.

Finally, invisible friends are really make-believe, aren't they? They may seem very real to us when we're small, but they actually come from our own imagination. Jesus is very real. Even though we can't see Jesus, we know he is with us. We can see his powerful love at work in the world. Because Jesus is real, and loves us, he is the best invisible friend any of us could have.

Let's Pray. Dear God, we thank you for our good friend Jesus, and for his presence with us. Amen.

Paul in Prison

Open Sesame

Props and Preparation Needed

1 Set of paper foot irons for each child (two large paper cuffs joined together by a smaller paper chain)

Tape and assistant jailers to help put the irons on the kids at the appropriate time.

1 Teenage or adult volunteer to play the role of jail keeper. Clue him or her into the part ahead of time.

1 Toy sword (can be made from corrugated cardboard covered with aluminum foil if a store-bought toy is unavailable)

1 Lantern, candle, or flashlight

The Message

I need your help to tell the story this morning, if you don't mind. I thought we'd act out the Bible story, kind of like a play. I will tell you what to do as we go along, okay?

The story takes place many years ago in an old Roman jail. Try to imagine yourself in a cold, dark place, with iron bars all around, and a big, heavy door with a strong lock on it right there. (*Point to imaginary door.*)

I would like all of you to pretend that you are prisoners in this jail. Here comes the jailer now, with his assistants, to put your legs in irons so you can't escape. (*If kids look frightened, you may reassure them, "Don't be afraid; remember, this is only a play." Have jailer and assistants mime opening the door, then closing it behind them with a "creak." They tape the paper irons around the children's ankles, and leave. If some don't want to participate, don't force them. Assistants go offstage. The jailer sits by the door and nods off to sleep.*)

There are two people in this prison who really don't belong here. They are named Paul and Silas. Would you like to be Paul, and you Silas? (*Assign two children the roles.*) Paul and Silas are Christians. They were arrested and thrown into jail even though they didn't do anything wrong.

It is now about midnight. The jailer is asleep by the door. Paul and Silas are praying and singing to God. The other prisoners are listening to them. Suddenly the whole jail is shaken by an earthquake. The prison door flies open, and the chains fall off all the prisoners' legs. Go ahead and pull your feet apart. Break those chains!

The guard wakes up. Now remember it's dark, and he can't see inside the cells. But he does see the door wide open. Naturally, he thinks all the prisoners have escaped. Rather than face the torture he knows is coming to him for allowing his prisoners to escape, he grabs his sword and is about to kill himself. (*Have guard mime the action as it is described.*) Paul shouts out from inside his cell, "No, stop! Don't hurt yourself! We are all here!"

The guard grabs a light and goes into the cells. The prisoners are still there! He finds Paul, kneels in front of him, and asks what he must do to be saved. The guard and all his family become Christians, and the church of Christ grows a little stronger.

Let's Pray. Dear God, we thank you for all the people of faith who have gone before us. Help us to learn from them how to be faithful people ourselves. Amen.

Acts 2:1–21

The Miracle of Understanding

Prop Needed

A German/English dictionary, or an electronic German/English dictionary, or a magazine ad that pictures either

A helium balloon, or a balloon tied to a plastic drinking straw for each child (optional)

The Message

In German: Guten Morgen, Knaben und Madchen! Wie gehts heute morgen? Habt Ihr ein Gutes Wochenende? Wer weisst was fur einen besonderen Tag heute fur die Kirche ist?

In English: Can't anyone answer that question? Wait a minute. What's wrong? (*Wait for answers.*) You can't understand what I'm saying? Why not?

Oh how silly of me! I was speaking German! German is the language people speak in the country of Germany. Most people who were born in, or have lived in, the United States for a long time speak English, don't they? People who live in different countries speak different languages. If we want to understand what someone from a different country is saying, we would have to learn her language, or she would have to learn ours. When you're trying to learn a new language, a dictionary like this one can be helpful. (*Show the children your dictionary or picture.*)

Suppose you wanted to know the German word for "church." You look up "church" in the dictionary, and it tells you that "church" in German is "Kirche."

The question I asked earlier was "Does anyone know what special day this is for the church, or kirche?" Today is Pentecost. Each year on Pentecost, we celebrate the church's birthday. Let me tell you why.

The church's first birthday took place a long, long time ago. It was after Jesus' resurrection, on the Jewish holiday of Pentecost. People from all over the world were gathered in Jerusalem for the big day, and they spoke many different languages. Jesus' followers were also in Jerusalem.

Suddenly there was a noise from the sky that sounded like a strong wind. It filled the house where the disciples and other believers were sitting. Then they saw something that looked like the flames from a fire go around the room and touch each person. Finally, Jesus' followers began to speak.

The loud windlike noise had been heard around the city. A large crowd gathered outside the house. When the disciples began to talk, the people from different countries could understand them, as if they were speaking each person's language. But those speaking were all from Galilee, and they didn't even have foreign language dictionaries with them!

The crowd didn't know how this could happen. How could they understand what was being said? "Those people must be drunk!" someone said. And then Peter stood up.

He spoke loudly as he explained that his friends were not drunk. No, what caused this miracle of understanding was the gift of God's Spirit. God sent the Holy Spirit to Jesus' followers that day, to unite them into what we call the church of Jesus Christ. We are a part of that church, and so today is our birthday too. Happy birthday, church!

Let's Pray. Dear God, we thank you for the gift of your Spirit. Thank you for this birthday celebration we call Pentecost. Amen.

(You may want to give each child a birthday balloon as he or she leaves.)

Season after Pentecost

H₂O and God

Props and Preparation Needed

1 Pitcher, filled with water, and a glass

1 Large piece of ice in a plastic bag

1 Thermos-type container filled with boiling water, with the cap on

The Message

This morning we are going to have a little science demonstration. We're going to explore the mysteries of hydrogen dioxide. Does anyone know a more common name for hydrogen dioxide? Sometimes we call it H_2O. What's another name for H_2O? (*Pause for answers.*) That's right—it's water!

(*Hold up pitcher and pour water into the glass as you say . . .*) H_2O in its liquid form is called water. H_2O comes in two other forms as well—a solid and a gas. What is the solid form of hydrogen dioxide called? (*Pause.*) Yes, ice! (*Hold up the piece of ice.*)

All things in the world are made up of tiny particles called molecules. These molecules move all the time. If liquid H_2O, or water, gets cold enough, as it does in a freezer, the molecules slow down so much that the water turns into a solid form that we called ice.

H_2O can also be a gas. If H_2O molecules get hot enough, as they can on a stove, they get so excited that they escape into the air and make steam. (*Remove lid from Thermos.*) Can everybody see the steam coming out of the Thermos bottle?

So H_2O is one substance in three forms—solid, liquid, and gas; or ice, water, and steam.

H_2O in its three forms can help us understand what God is like. God is one being, or one personality, in three forms.

There is God, the heavenly Parent. In this form, God created the world and everything in it. God created the stars and the moon, the plants and the animals, you and me. God the Parent loves us as a father or mother, wants to take care of us, and hopes for our love in return.

We also know God in the form of the Son, Jesus. People had forgotten what it meant to be a child of God. So Jesus came to remind us and to save us. God came into the world in the form of Jesus, so that we could all be brought back to God.

The third form in which we know God is the Holy Spirit. Through the Holy Spirit, God is with us always. Through the Holy Spirit we experience God's love in our lives.

So God, like H_2O, can be found in three forms—Parent, Son, and Holy Spirit. When you put all three forms together, we call God the Trinity. Can you say that? The Trinity—God: Parent, Son, and Holy Spirit.

Let's Pray. Dear God, sometimes you are hard to understand. Help us to keep trying though, and help us to recognize you when we find you. Amen.

On Fire for the Lord

Props and Preparation Needed

Two new candles. Remove any trace of wax from the wick of one candle by scraping it with a knife. Soak the exposed wick in a glass of water.

Matches

The Message

Let's try a science experiment. I have here two candles, exactly the same except this one is soaking in water, and this one isn't. (*Show the candles, one in the glass of water upside-down.*) *John*, will you please hold this candle for me while I light it? (*Hand the dry candle to an older child.*) Hold it still and straight up, okay? (*Light the candle.*) That was easy, wasn't it? It lit right away. *John*, you may blow the candle out. Thank you for your help.

Now we'll light the other candle. *Nellie*, would you please hold this candle for me, straight and still just like John did? (*Hand wet candle to another child.*) I'll just light the match, hold it up to the wick, and we should have a pretty candle flame. (*Attempt to light the candle.*) But the candle won't light. Why do you think it won't light? (*Listen to answers.*) That's right! The wick is all wet! You can't light a wet candle, just like you can't use wet wood to make a fire. Water makes it very hard or impossible to light a fire. Remember our experiment while I tell you this morning's story.

Elijah was a prophet of God thousands of years ago. God sent Elijah to talk to the people of Israel because they were forgetting their own God and worshiping Baal, the god their neighbors worshiped. Elijah knew that Baal was not real. A false god is called an idol. Baal was an idol.

Elijah went to King Ahab. He told Ahab to have all the prophets of Baal and all the people of Israel meet him on Mount Carmel. Everyone did what the king told them to do. The four hundred prophets of Baal were there. All the Israelites were there on the mountain. And Elijah was there. Elijah challenged the prophets of Baal to a contest to prove whose God was real—Baal or the Lord.

Two bulls were brought for sacrifices. When animal sacrifices were made, the animals were killed and cut up and cooked on an altar made of stones and wood. Elijah challenged Baal's prophets to light the fire for the sacrifice without a flame. They were to pray to their god. If Baal sent a flame to light the fire, then Baal was a real god.

The prophets set up the altar with the butchered bull on top. Then they started to pray. They prayed and prayed. They chanted. They danced around the altar. "Answer us, Baal," they shouted, but no answer came.

After several hours, Elijah started to tease the prophets of Baal. "Maybe you should pray louder," he said. "Maybe your god can't hear you." So they prayed even louder. They ranted and raved until they were exhausted. Still no answer came.

Then it was Elijah's turn. He fixed the altar of the Lord, which had been torn down. He piled up twelve stones. He dug a trench around the altar and piled wood on top of the stones. He put the butchered bull on top of the wood. Then he did something very strange. He had the people fill four jars with water and poured it over everything—the bull, the wood, and the stones. He did this three times, until the water ran down and filled the trench. Everything was soaking wet. Then Elijah prayed to his God, the God of Israel.

God answered Elijah's prayer. The Lord sent down fire. Even though the altar, the wood, and the meat were totally drenched, God's fire burned up the sacrifice, the wood, and the altar. The fire scorched the ground and even dried up all the water in the trench.

The people got the point. They bowed down and worshiped the Lord again. "The Lord God of Israel is the only true God," they said.

Let's Pray. Dear God, help us to be your faithful followers, even when it is not a popular thing to do. In Jesus' name. Amen.

God's Brave Messengers

Props Needed

A Chinese fortune cookie that contains a prediction, such as "Great wealth is coming your way," rather than a proverb

1 Fortune cookie for each child (optional)

The Message

How many of you like Chinese food? Sweet and sour pork, cashew chicken, egg rolls? I'm making myself hungry! I think going out for Chinese food is fun. Not only does everything taste so good, but what do you always get for dessert? (*Pause for answers.*) Right! A fortune cookie!

I just happen to have a fortune cookie with me this morning. (*Bring out your cookie.*) Shall we see what my fortune is? (*Break open cookie and read the fortune.*) It says, "You will win the lottery." That's a pretty good fortune! Do you think it will come true? Maybe. But if the fortune did come true, would it be because I got this fortune cookie? No. Fortunes told in fortune cookies are really just a fun game, aren't they? They can't make things happen.

I'm going to switch gears now and ask if anyone knows what a prophet is. (*Pause.*) We read about prophets mostly in the Old Testament of the Bible. Many people think that prophets were fortune tellers, kind of like the cookies. They think that the prophets' main purpose was to predict what would happen in the future. This is not really a good explanation of the prophets' job.

Prophets were men and women chosen by God to give the king or the people of Israel a message. Prophets told folks what God wanted them to do.

Being a prophet was hard. In fact, most of the really important prophets tried to turn down the job when God first chose them. Usually the message God wanted the prophets to deliver was not a happy one. God didn't usually send a prophet unless something needed to be changed. Often the message was "Return to God and start following God's law again, or you and your nation will be destroyed."

As you can imagine, delivering a message like this didn't make the prophets very popular. Sometimes they would become discouraged when the people didn't listen to them and do what God wanted. Sometimes their lives were threatened. But God always gave them the strength and courage they needed to obey God and do their job. Some of the most famous prophets were Elijah, Isaiah, Jeremiah, Hosea, Amos, Deborah, and Jonah.

Let's Pray. Dear God, we thank you for your prophets and the important work they did. Give us the same strength and courage to follow wherever you may lead us. Amen.

All People Created Equal

Props Needed
Flannel board
Flannel-board figures (found in the Appendix)

The Message
Good morning. Do any of you know what you want to be when you grow up? (*Listen to children's answers.*) Those are all very interesting things to be!

I have some pictures of people to show you. I'll put them up on the flannel board, and you tell me what each person's job is, okay? Here's the first picture. What is this person? A doctor, right. (*Put all the pictures on the board, one at a time. Help the children if they cannot easily identify the figure's occupation.*)

So we have a doctor, a construction worker, a business executive, a police officer, and a minister. These people do different jobs, but they all have something in common. Can you tell me what that is? They are all women! These women are all doing jobs that used to be done only by men.

Until very recently, women were not allowed to be doctors or construction workers or ministers. Only men could be business executives or police officers or professional athletes. Even today it is sometimes harder for women than men in these professions. But if you want it badly enough, and work hard enough, any of you can be whatever you choose when you grow up.

Jesus lived nearly two thousand years ago. He was always doing things that made the religious leaders upset and angry. He healed people on the Sabbath, when no one was supposed to work. He ate dinner with people who were considered bad. And he treated women with respect.

You see, in Jesus' time most men did not think women were really very important. But Jesus knew that this was not how God wanted things to be. Jesus knew that God created men and women to be equal partners in life—one just as important as the other. So Jesus treated women with respect.

Some of Jesus' closest friends and helpers in his ministry were women. Some of Jesus' strongest supporters were women too. They helped Jesus and his disciples could travel and share the good news of God's love and forgiveness.

The world today is a lot different than it was when Jesus was on earth. We hope that today we are getting closer to Jesus' example of treating all people with equal respect and consideration.

Let's Pray. Great and wonderful God, we thank you for sending your son, Jesus, to show us the way to live. Help us to follow his example. Amen.

God's Still, Small Voice

Prop Needed

The children, helping you to tell the story

The Message

A couple of weeks ago we talked about God's special messengers. Do you remember what these men and women are called? (*Pause for answer.*) They are called prophets. Prophets are people who share the Lord's message with God's people. Today I'm going to tell you about God's prophet Elijah.

You remember I told you that prophets were not always popular people. Often the message God had for the people was something that they didn't want to hear, and they often blamed the prophet for the message. This was true in Elijah's case. In fact, obeying God had gotten Elijah into so much trouble that the queen of Israel, Jezebel, threatened to kill him. Elijah didn't know what to do, so he ran for his life.

He ended up at Mount Sinai—God's holy mountain. This was the place where the Lord gave Moses the Ten Commandments. Elijah hoped to find God there. Elijah was not disappointed. God told Elijah to stand on top of the mountain and wait. Elijah did what God told him.

Up on that mountain, a huge, roaring gust of wind blew by Elijah. Can you help me make the sound of the wind? (*Make wind sounds and wave your arms from side to side, giving the impression of wind. Stop, and when everyone is quiet, say:*) But God was not in the wind.

Next came an earthquake. The ground shook (*shake as if in an earthquake, and encourage kids to do the same*), and the trees swayed. (*When quiet again, say:*) But God was not in the earthquake.

After the earthquake there was a fire. How does fire feel? Hot! Whew! (*Wipe your brow.*) But God was not in the fire.

After the fire, there was silence. In the silence, Elijah heard God say, "Elijah, what are you doing here?" Elijah poured out his heart to God. He told God how, even though he had done everything God had told him to do, the people of Israel would not listen. They killed God's prophets, and Jezebel wanted him dead too.

In the still quiet of that mountaintop, God told Elijah how to straighten out the mess. Sometimes we can learn a lot if we just stop for a moment and are quiet.

Let's Pray. Dear God, in our noisy and crowded lives, help us to take time out to be quiet and to listen for your guidance. Amen.

Love Is . . .

Prop Needed
A tricycle covered with a sheet or tablecloth

The Message
Hi, everybody. I have something to show you this morning that I think you'll all recognize. (*Remove cover from tricycle.*) You know what it is? A tricycle, of course!

How many of you have a tricycle at home? How many of you used to ride a tricycle before graduating to a two-wheeler? Does anyone know why this kind of bike is called a tricycle? (*Pause.*) *Tri* means "three," and *cycle* means "wheels." A bike with three wheels is called a tricycle. Today's story is about a boy, a girl, and a tricycle.

Mrs. Tucker was waiting for her daughter, Kathy, to come home for lunch. Kathy was seven years old and was playing at a neighbor's house. Mrs. Tucker had told her to be home by twelve o'clock, and it was now twelve-thirty. Mrs. Tucker was beginning to worry. Kathy had never been this late before. She picked up the phone to call the neighbor, when her daughter walked through the kitchen door.

"Kathy, where have you been?" her mother asked. "I was beginning to worry!"

"I'm sorry I'm late, Mom," Kathy answered. "But on my way home, I saw Jimmy Meyers standing on the sidewalk, crying. The wheel was broken on his tricycle. I stopped to help him."

Kathy's mother looked confused. "I didn't realize you knew how to fix a tricycle!" she said. "Where did you get the tools?"

"I didn't help Jimmy fix the wheel," explained Kathy. "I helped him to cry."

The Bible tells us that because God loves us, we should love one another. One way we can show our love for other people is by helping them—helping Mom or Dad with chores around the house, pulling weeds in the yard, helping our younger brothers or sisters get dressed, putting our toys away. We can help older people, like our grandparents or neighbors, by bringing them things they need or by keeping them company. We can help our friends with a project or with a problem. And sometimes we can show our love for other people by helping them laugh or helping them cry.

Let's Pray. Dear God, we thank you for the love and help you give to us. May we love and help our family and friends. Amen.

Seventy-Two Plus You

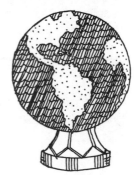

Props Needed
A globe
2 Small stickers

The Message

I brought a globe in to show you this morning. A globe is a round map of the world. Can anyone show me where the United States is on this globe? (*Have a volunteer point out the United States. If no one can, you point to it.*) Good! This big area right here is our country. Now can anyone find our state on the globe? Where is Oregon (*use your own state*)? Very good. Our town is right about here. (*Place a sticker where your town would be.*)

Now I have a tougher question. Can anyone locate the country of Israel on the globe? (*Give opportunity for someone to volunteer.*) Here it is, way over here on the other side of the world from us. And here is Jerusalem, where Jesus spent quite a bit of time and was finally crucified. (*Mark Jerusalem with a sticker.*)

Have you ever wondered how the news about Jesus spread from this one tiny spot, across the entire globe, all the way to Woodburn, Oregon (*use your own town and state*)? Remember, at the time of Jesus there were no televisions, no radios, no telephones, no printing presses, no FAX machines, or computers! How did the word about Jesus and his teachings get around and spread so far?

Jesus started with the twelve disciples. They helped Jesus in his work, learned from him, and told others about him. As Jesus traveled about, teaching and healing, news about him spread. One person told another person, who told another person what he or she had seen or heard. Then Jesus called together seventy-two people. He sent them out ahead of him to different towns and villages to tell the people he was coming. He sent them out to tell the people that the kingdom of God was near.

After Jesus' death and resurrection his followers branched out even farther. They traveled to different countries, spreading the good news about Jesus and starting churches. Eventually word got around, so that today Christians can be found almost everywhere in the world.

There are still some people in the world who have not heard about Jesus. There are people in other countries, and in the United States, who have never heard the good news. So even today, our church sends out people to spread the news about Jesus. These people are called missionaries.

You can be a missionary here in Woodburn (*use your town*) too. If you have a friend who doesn't have a church home, you can invite your friend to church with you so that he or she will come to know and love Jesus also.

Let's Pray. Dear God, we thank you that we have this church where we learn about you. Help our church to spread the good news about Jesus, our Savior. Amen.

Good Sam

Prop Needed
None

The Message

Do you know who your neighbors are? Do you know their names? Do you play with your neighbors sometimes? Today's story answers the question "Who is my neighbor?"

Once a teacher of the law asked Jesus what he must do to receive eternal life—how could he get to heaven? Jesus asked the man, "What do the Scriptures say?" The man answered, " 'Love the Lord your God with all your soul, with all your strength, and with all your mind,' and 'Love your neighbor as yourself.' "

"You are right," Jesus said. "Do this, and you will go to heaven."

The man asked Jesus, "Who is my neighbor?" Jesus then told him this story.

Once there was a Jewish man who was going down from Jerusalem to Jericho. All of a sudden, robbers sprang out from behind the rocks. They attacked the man, beat him, took his clothes and money, and left him on the road to die.

A short time later a priest came by. Priests were kind of like ministers. The priest thought of himself as a very religious person. But when he saw the bleeding man on the road, he didn't help him. He just kept walking.

Next a Levite came by. Levites were people who helped the priests in the Temple. So the Levite was considered to be a very good, religious person also. But did he help the beaten man on the road? No! He just kept walking.

The next person to walk down the road was a Samaritan. The Samaritans and the Jews were bitter enemies. They didn't eat together or play together or even talk to one another. You wouldn't expect the Samaritan to help the injured Jewish man, would you? But he did.

He saw the man crumpled on the ground, and he felt very sorry for him. He cleaned his sores and put bandages on them. The Samaritan put the man on his mule and took him to an inn where he took care of him overnight. The next day he gave the innkeeper money from his own pocket and asked that the man be cared for until he was well.

Jesus ended the story by asking the teacher, "Who do you think was a neighbor to the man attacked by robbers?" What do you think? Who was the good neighbor in the story? Was it the priest, who walked right by the man? Was it the Levite, who ignored the man and kept walking? Or was the neighbor the Samaritan, who was kind to the beaten man? (*Pause for answers.*) That's right, it was the Samaritan.

Our neighbors aren't only the people who live next door or across the street. A neighbor is someone who shows kindness to others, no matter who they are or where they come from.

Jesus then told the teacher, "Go and show kindness as the Samaritan did."

Let's Pray. Dear God, thank you for the lessons we learn from the Bible. Help us to be kind to others. Amen.

What's the Message?

Prop Needed

A piece of paper with a secret message written on it

The Message

This morning we're going to start our time together with a game. Have any of you ever played "Telephone"? It is a simple game. I'm going to whisper a secret message into someone's ear. Then that person will whisper exactly the same message into the next person's ear. We'll pass the message around until everyone has heard it and told it to the person next to him or her. The last one to hear the secret will then tell the congregation what it is, okay? Here's the message. (*Read the message from the paper. If you only have a few children, you may want to pass the message through a pew or two of the congregation too, so that it has a chance to become garbled.*)

Okay, Billy (*use real names*) what's the message? (*Allow the last child to share the message.*) Really? Is that what you heard? Is that what all of you heard? No? What was the message when you heard it? (*Point to someone in the middle of the telephone line.*) Here is what I read to the first person. (*Read the message.*) The message sure changed, didn't it! How did it get so messed up? (*Pause for answers.*)

That's right. Each person heard the message changed just a little bit. Everyone didn't hear it quite right, and so the message each passed on was slightly different from the last time. With each person changing it just a little bit, the message was completely different by the end.

Gossip works the same way. I might tell you something I heard about someone else—for example, "Bobby got a C on his spelling test." You might pass along the story to another friend, saying Bobby got a D on his math quiz. You don't mean to lie. You just make a little mistake when you pass on the message. Finally, someone might come up to Bobby and say, "Hey, I heard you flunked second grade and have to go to summer school!"

Gossip and rumors almost always hurt people. Most often rumors aren't true, but even if a rumor is true, people don't like to have others talking about them behind their backs. If you hear a rumor, the best thing to do is ignore it. Don't make it worse by telling someone else what you heard.

Let's Pray. Dear God, you give us life to take care of each other, not to hurt one another. Help us to treat each other with love and respect. Amen.

"Now I Lay Me Down to Sleep"

Prop Needed

A book of children's prayers

The Message

I have a book I want to show you this morning. (*Hold up book.*) It is a special book for children. It is a book filled with prayers.

Who can tell me what prayer is? (*Pause for answers.*) That's right—prayer is talking with God. Let me read a couple of these prayers to you. (*Read one or two prayers from the book.*)

We say a prayer at the end of each children's story in our morning worship, don't we? Do you pray at other times too? (*Listen to children's answers.*) We pray at other times during the service of worship and in church school. Someone mentioned saying grace before supper. Grace is a prayer we say to thank God for our food. How many people say their prayers before they go to bed? Do you use fancy prayers like the ones in this book, or do you just tell God what's on your mind?

God likes us to pray, to share our thoughts and feelings. God doesn't care whether we use fancy, memorized prayers or whether we use our own words. It makes God happy when we take time out to tell God how we're doing.

If you had a friend who never talked to you, how would you feel about that person? He or she wouldn't be a very good friend, right? Well, God is our friend, and we need to communicate with the Lord, just as we do with our other friends. God wants to know from us when we're feeling sad, or lonely, or frightened, or happy.

One really neat thing about prayer is that you can do it anytime and anyplace. You don't have to fold your hands and bow your head each time you pray. Sometimes a simple "Thanks, God" when something good has happened, or a "Help!" when you're in trouble, is all it takes to let God know how you're doing.

Let's Pray. Dear God, we are glad that you care about us. As we go about our busy days of playing, school, study, eating, help us to remember to take time out to share with you. Amen.

The Case of the Greedy Dog

Prop Needed
A dog bone

The Message

Have you ever wanted something you didn't really need? Maybe your best friend just got the latest Nintendo game or a bike in a hot new color. If you ask your parents about getting one too, they may say something like, "You already have enough Nintendo games" or "There's nothing wrong with the bike we bought you last year." Our story this morning is about wanting more than you need, or greed.

Once upon a time, a dog was trotting down the road with a happy look on his face. The dog was smiling because he had a nice juicy bone in his mouth. It was not an enormous bone, but then he was not an enormous dog. The bone would make a very tasty meal for the dog indeed.

The dog was going to his favorite shady spot across the river to enjoy his lunch. He came to the fallen tree that formed a bridge and started to walk across to the cool shade on the other side. When he reached the middle of the log, the dog glanced down into the water. He stopped in his tracks. "What is this?" he thought to himself. "Another dog. And his bone is bigger than mine!"

The dog on the log decided that he wanted the other dog's bone instead of his own. He tried to snatch the bone from the other dog's mouth. In trying to bite the other bone, his own bone fell into the water. All the dog got for his trouble was a wet face. For what he had seen in the water was not a dog with a bigger bone at all. What he saw in the water was his own reflection.

Jesus said, "Take care! Be on your guard against all kinds of greed; for one's life does not consist in the abundance of possessions." (Luke 12:15).

It's easy to get caught up in wanting to have a lot of things—especially when our friends have them. But Jesus, and the dog in the story, teach us that who we are on the inside is much more important than what we own.

Let's Pray. Good and generous God, help us not to long for things we don't need, and help us to share what we do have with those who have less. In Jesus' name we pray. Amen.

Praise the Lord!

Prop Needed
A church bulletin showing the Order of Worship

The Message
Good morning, boys and girls! I am happy to see all of you this morning. Do you know why all of us are here? Why are we all together in this sanctuary every Sunday, rather than outside playing ball or watching TV or at a picnic? (*Pause for answers.*)

We are here to worship God. Once a week we take time out of our busy schedules to come together as a community of faith in worship. We thank God for all the good things we have received, and we tell the Lord how much we appreciate who God is and what God does in the world. We also learn more about God and how we should live as Christians. And sometimes we ask God for help with our problems.

How do we do all these things? How do we worship? We worship God in many different ways. The church bulletin (*show bulletin*) is a helpful tool that lists all the different ways we worship. Let's look at today's Order of Worship for a minute.

There are some prayers listed. Some are printed here. Everybody who can read says the printed prayers together. Some prayers have only a heading, like this one. It says, "The Pastoral Prayer." That prayer is spoken for the people by the pastor.

What's another way we worship besides prayer? (*Pause for answers.*) Yes, we listen to music throughout the service, and we sing hymns ourselves too. Some hymns are prayers that we sing to God. Other hymns are songs about God or the church.

We hear God's Word read to us in the Scripture lessons. Then the pastor explains the Scriptures in the sermon. Sometimes we learn about God. Some sermons teach us how God wants us to live our lives. Our time together is the same thing, isn't it? We learn about God and how to be good Christians.

One way we thank God for all we have been given is through our offering. We give money each week to thank God for our blessings by helping others.

Sometimes we stand during worship, and sometimes we sit. By standing and sitting, we worship God with our bodies as well as with our minds and voices. (*If your congregation sometimes uses applause, liturgical dance, or the passing of the peace, mention them here.*)

The most important way we worship is with our hearts. This means that we are sincere in what we're doing here. We really mean it when we praise and thank God in our prayers, our songs, our offerings, our listening. When we worship with our hearts our worship is real, and God feels our love.

Let's Pray. Dear God, we come to worship you because we love you. Thank you for being our God and allowing us to be your people. Amen.

Switched-on Christians

Props Needed

Several ownership manuals for various appliances
(Adjust your message to your own manuals.)
A Bible

The Message

Good morning, boys and girls! I have with me this morning several ownership manuals. You get one of these little booklets every time you buy an appliance. (*Show the manuals.*) Here's one for a dishwasher. Here's the manual for a TV, a VCR, a can opener, and a stereo.

An ownership manual tells you how the machine works. It tells you how to set it up. For example the stereo manual shows where all the different wires are supposed to be connected. (*Show this picture from the manual.*) The ownership manual also has a section in the back called "Troubleshooting." If something isn't working right, the troubleshooting section offers suggestions on how to correct the problem. For example, here it says that if your stereo won't turn on—if you press the power button and nothing happens—the first thing you should do is check to be sure it's plugged into the power source. You should check to make sure it's plugged into the wall socket.

Wouldn't it be great if life came with an ownership manual? If there were a booklet that told us how we are supposed to live, what to do with all the different parts of our lives, and what to do when things go wrong?

Well, God, the manufacturer who gave us our lives, also gives us an ownership manual. It is called the Bible. (*Hold up the Bible.*)

The Bible gives us instructions on how to live. The Bible also offers suggestions on how to solve problems in our lives—what to do when things go wrong. There may not be specific answers to each individual question you may have, but there are general answers that will help you with any problem. Love one another. Be honest; don't cheat others. Help those in trouble, and so on.

Most important, the Bible teaches us how to stay plugged into God, our source of power and life. A stereo or a refrigerator or any appliance will not work unless it's plugged into its power source, electricity. Our lives won't work right unless we're plugged into God. We get our power and strength from God, kind of like the way an appliance gets its power from electricity. Without God, we would be as useless as a broken Nintendo game.

Let's Pray. Dear God, we know that without you, we can do nothing. Thank you for giving us your Word in the Bible so we can learn how to stay plugged into you, our source of power and life. In Jesus' name we pray. Amen.

Unpopular Choices

Props Needed
An apple
A bag of small candies

The Message

Hi! I have two snacks with me this morning—a big shiny apple and a bag of candy. (*Hold up snacks.*) If I were to offer you one of these, which one would you choose? How many of you would choose the apple? Raise your hands. How many would choose the candy?

Which of these two foods is more healthful for your body? Which one will help you to grow? And you would still choose the candy, even though it's not really good for you? Well, that's okay. A little candy every once in a while won't hurt you as long as you eat healthful food most of the time. Sometimes the choices we are asked to make are a little more serious than deciding what food to eat. And sometimes making the wrong choice really can hurt us.

Jeremiah was a prophet who lived thousands of years ago. The message that God had Jeremiah deliver to the people of Israel did not make him a very popular person. He told them that God was very angry with their evil ways and if they didn't change, they would be destroyed.

The more Jeremiah obeyed God by giving them God's message, the angrier the people got. They called Jeremiah names, they harassed, beat, and more than once almost killed him. Jeremiah felt terrible! He thought about ignoring God himself, so that the people would leave him alone. Jeremiah had a choice to make:

obey God and be unpopular with the people, or ignore God, be quiet, and make the people happy. Jeremiah decided he'd rather be at peace with God than make the people happy. He continued to be God's prophet, preaching God's message, and getting into trouble.

As you grow older, you will be faced with some tough choices. Sometimes people will want you to do something that you know is wrong. It might involve cigarettes or alcohol, drugs, or stealing. They might laugh at you or call you names if you refuse to go along with them and say no.

When you're faced with a hard decision like that, ask yourself, "What would God want me to do?" And remember that it's always better to be friends with God than to be popular with other people. In making healthy choices, you'll also be a better friend to yourself.

Let's Pray. Dear God, sometimes we are faced with really hard decisions. Help us to make the right choices in our lives. Amen.

Praise with Shouts of Joy

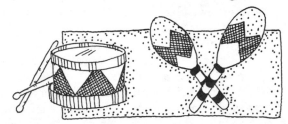

Props Needed
A Bible

Assorted rhythm instruments (If you don't have access to rhythm instruments, you can make your own or use pots, pans, and utensils from the kitchen.)

The Message
Good morning, boys and girls. This morning we're going to talk about noise. Do you ever think much about noise? Do grown-ups ever tell you, "Stop making so much noise! I can't hear myself think!"

Actually, noise is a very important part of our lives. Certain noises cause us to do certain things. An alarm clock tells us it's time to get up. A siren tells us, "Get out of the way! A fire truck is coming!" We listen for cars when we cross the street, as well as watch for them. People who are deaf and cannot hear sounds have to be very careful. They cannot hear the warnings around them, such as sirens or someone shouting, "Watch out!"

Different noises can make us feel different ways too. Crying is most often a sad sound, isn't it? Can you think of other sad noises? What kind of noise would a creaking door in the middle of the night be? Maybe scary. The howling wind can be a scary sound too. What are some happy noises? (*Pause for answers.*)

The Bible tells us,

> Shout for joy to God our defender;
> sing praise to the God of Jacob!
> —Psalm 81:1, TEV

A joyful noise is a happy noise. The Bible tells us to make happy noises to God, even in church. What happy noises have you heard in church? (*Children may need help with some suggestions: laughing, a baby talking, happy words, clapping, organ playing, singing.*) Music is one way we make joyful noises to the Lord each Sunday.

I want to teach you a song this morning. It's called "Rejoice in the Lord Always." That means, "Be happy in God." It goes like this . . . (*Teach the children the song.*)

Re - joice in the Lord   al - ways, and a - gain I say, "Re-joice!"

Re - joice!   Re - joice!   And a - gain   I   say, "Re - joice!"

That sounded pretty good, but I think our song needs to be noisier. This time, clap your hands as you sing. (*Sing song again.*)

Better. We're getting better. But I think that to make a truly joyful noise, we need more *volume.* (*Pass out rhythm instruments.*) Here, everybody take an instrument. We'll sing the song one more time. Play your instrument as you sing. Give it all you've got. Let's make a joyful noise to the Lord! (*Sing.*)

Terrific!

Let's Pray. God, we praise you. We praise you with our noise and in our silence, with our good deeds and our kind thoughts. We praise you, God, because we love you. Amen.

God and Air

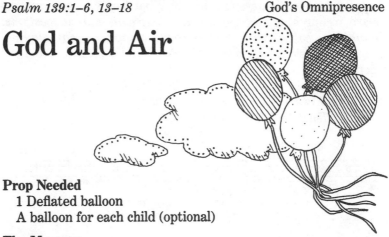

Prop Needed
1 Deflated balloon
A balloon for each child (optional)

The Message

Good morning! Here we are this morning, worshiping God in this beautiful church. Another word for this part of the church is the "sanctuary." Sometimes the church is also called "God's house." Have you ever heard the church called God's house before?

God's house. God is here in this place, with us. But God doesn't live in the church building as you and I live in our houses or apartments. God is here, and God is everywhere. That's sort of a hard idea to understand at first, isn't it—the idea that God is everywhere? But it's true. God is a spirit. God doesn't have a body, as you and I have. We can be in only one place at a time, can't we? But because God is a Spirit, the Lord can be everywhere at once.

It's kind of like air. Air is all around us and even in us. We breathe air; it helps keep us alive. We can't see air though, can we? But we know it is here. We can't see the air itself, but we can see what air does. Now watch this. (*Blow up the balloon.*) We can't actually see the air, but we can see that it has made the balloon bigger. We cannot see God, but we know that God is here, and everywhere, just like air. We can see the good in people and in the world, and we know that God is with us.

God also knows us, even better than we know ourselves. God knows what we like and what we don't like, how we feel, who our friends are, whether we've been cooperative or naughty. The Lord even knows how many hairs are on your head!

We might not like the idea of God's being all around us and knowing so much about us. It's kind of creepy, except for one thing. God loves us—better than anybody. And that makes God a welcome friend to have around.

Let's Pray. Good God, we thank you for your presence with us. Help us not to disappoint you too often and forgive us when we do. In Jesus' name we pray. Amen.

(You may want to give the children each a balloon as they leave.)

Lost Dog

Prop and Preparation Needed

A "Lost Dog" poster (Make a poster like those posted on telephone poles, appealing for the return of a lost dog.)

The Message

Have any of you ever lost your dog or cat? Maybe the dog dug a hole under your fence and went exploring. Or maybe the cat wandered off while you were gone for the weekend.

What is the first thing you would do if you discovered that your pet was missing? (*Pause for answers.*) You would look for it, wouldn't you? First you'd probably search the house . . . check behind all the closet doors and in the basement to make sure your pet hadn't gotten trapped somewhere by mistake. If you couldn't find it in the house, you'd probably check the yard and the garage. Still no sign of it. The next step might be to ask the neighbors if they had seen your dog or cat. Then you'd start to search the neighborhood. You and others in your family might walk up and down the streets, calling your pet's name. If you're older you might ride your bike all over the neighborhood, calling for your pet. If you still couldn't find it on foot or on your bike, someone might take you in the car so you could look farther away from home. After looking for several hours, you might finally make posters like this one (*show the poster*) and put them around the neighborhood in hopes that someone would find your pet and return it. (*Read the poster.*)

How would you feel if your dog or cat were lost? (*Listen to answers.*) And what if, after several days, someone called to say they had found Buster, and could you come pick him up? How would you feel then? (*Pause.*) You would feel very, very happy, wouldn't you? You would want to celebrate your pet's return home.

The Bible tells us that is how God feels every time another person decides to follow Jesus. When people choose to stop living only for themselves and to start putting God first in their lives, it makes God very, very happy. All of heaven celebrates, because it is as though a person has been lost, and now has been found. That person has returned to the family of God.

Let's Pray. God, who seeks the lost, we are glad that you care so much about us. Thank you for making a special place for each one of us in the family of God. Amen.

A Good Feeling

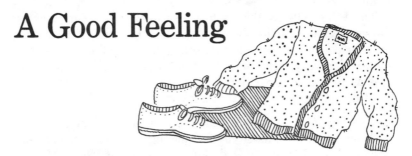

Props and Preparation Needed

A cardigan sweater

A pair of ordinary canvas sneakers, not athletic shoes

If you've never seen it, watch one episode of "Mister Rogers' Neighborhood."

The Message

Whom do you know from TV, who begins every program by going to his closet, taking off his jacket, putting on a sweater, and then changing from his dress shoes into his comfy sneakers? (*You may want to change into these casual clothes yourself, or just hold each item up for the kids to see as you mention it. Pause for answers.*)

Mr. Rogers, that's right! How many of you watch Mr. Rogers or used to watch him when you were younger? Mr. Rogers always brings something with him to show you, doesn't he? That's kind of like what we do here each Sunday. Sometimes he makes things or shows a movie about how people make things in factories. Sometimes Mr. Rogers builds with blocks or experiments in the sand. There's always a portion of the show spent in the Neighborhood of Make-Believe. Who are some of the people who live there? (King Friday, Princess Sara, Lady Aberlin, Lady Elaine Fairchilde, Daniel Tiger, X the Owl, Cornflake S. Specially, Bob Dog, and others.) And Mr. Rogers always remembers to feed his fish. What's your very favorite part of that television visit? (*Listen to answers.*)

My favorite part is the very end. Mr. Rogers has changed back into his work clothes—his jacket and dress shoes. Just before he goes out the door he turns to his television friends and says, "You make each day a special day. You know how; by just your being you. There is no one else in the world exactly like you. And people can like you just the way you are."

"I like you just the way you are." Doesn't it feel good when someone says that to you? "I like you just the way you are—even though you sometimes make mistakes or can't do some things as well as the bigger kids. That's okay. You're special, and I like you just the way you are."

Mr. Rogers isn't the only one who likes us just the way we are. God does too. God's love for us never stops, even if we make mistakes or do something we shouldn't do. God can be disappointed if we are naughty on purpose and wants us to try our best to be good. But God also forgives us when we're wrong and loves us all the time. I think that knowing that God loves us and always will, is a very good feeling.

Let's Pray. Dear God, we thank you for friends like Mr. Rogers who remind us of your love and who help us to feel good about ourselves. Thank you for loving us without fail. Amen.

The Root of All Evil?

Props Needed
10 Dimes for each child

The Message

Can anyone tell me what an allowance is? (*Listen to answers.*) Yes, an allowance is an amount of money some children get from their parents each week or each month. How many of you get an allowance? What do you do with your allowance? (*Listen to answers.*) Why does your mom or dad give you an allowance? (*Listen to answers.*) I'll bet one reason your folks give you an allowance is so that you will learn how to handle money.

In the Bible a lot is written about money and what we should do with it. Money can be a useful, good thing. We need money to buy clothes and food and to pay for a place to live. But money can also be a very dangerous thing if we let having lots and lots of money become too important to us.

Money is like fire. Fire can be good. We can use fire to heat our homes, cook our food, light birthday candles, or to sing around when we're camping. But fire can be a very dangerous thing if it gets out of hand or is used the wrong way. How many of you have ever burned yourselves? It hurts, doesn't it? Fire can destroy buildings and forests and can burn people, too, if we're not very careful with it. Fire, and money, can be used in helpful ways or in hurtful ways.

The Bible has a saying in it, "The love of money is the root of all evil." Not money itself, but the love of money. People who can think only about getting rich become very selfish. They might even lie or cheat or steal to get more money. This is what "the root of all evil" means.

God does not want money to be the most important thing in our lives. Loving God and helping others is much more important than getting rich. We can use our money to show our love for God by helping others. We can share part of what we have with those who don't have as much. One way we can do that is by giving money to the church. The church takes part of the offering each week and shares it with those in need. There are other groups that help needy people that you could share with too.

I am going to give each one of you a dollar. (*Give each child ten dimes.*) This is not a dollar bill. It's ten dimes. It is the same amount of money as a dollar bill, but it's in coins. This is your money. You may do whatever you want with it. You may want to spend some of it. Maybe you'll want to save some in your piggy bank. You might choose to help others with some of your money. Or you may decide to just blow the whole dollar on something you really want. It's up to you.

Let's Pray. Dear God, you give us so much—family, friends, a church, the earth, school, life itself. Help us to be responsible and generous with what we have been given. Amen.

The Little Engine That Could

Prop Needed

A copy of the children's picture book *The Little Engine That Could* (This book can be easily obtained at the public library or at any bookstore that handles children's books.)

The Message

Good morning, boys and girls! Today I want to read you a story you may have heard before. It's called *The Little Engine That Could*. Who has heard this story? It's a good one, isn't it? Okay, here we go with *The Little Engine That Could*.

(Read the story, showing the children the pictures. You may want to hold the book in your lap, facing the children, and read it upside down.)

The little engine wasn't sure at first whether she could make it over the mountain, was she? She did something very brave. She decided to try anyway.

Sometimes we don't know what we can do until we try. And with God's help, anything is possible.

Let's Pray. Dear God, help us to be brave like the little engine. May we try to do new things, knowing that you are with us to help us succeed. Amen.

On Giving Thanks

Props Needed

A gift you have received recently—adapt the story to reflect your gift

A Thank-you note

Flannel board

Flannel-board figures (found in the Appendix)

The Message

On my last birthday, my mother gave me this shirt I'm wearing. I like it very much. It was nice of my mother to remember my birthday and to give me a present. To tell her how much I appreciated her thinking of me, I sent her a thank-you note like this one. It has the words "Thank You" printed on the outside in fancy letters. The inside of the card is blank. That's where I wrote my note. I told my mom how much I liked the shirt and that it fit just right. I thanked her for sending it to me.

How many of you have written thank-you notes, or told your mom or dad what to write, to someone who has given you a present or done something nice for you? People like to know that you received their gift and that you appreciated it.

Jesus once gave a very special gift to ten men. Let's listen and see if they remembered to say thank you.

Jesus was walking into a village when he heard ten people call out to him, "Jesus! Master! Help us!" (*Follow story with flannel-board figures.*) The men had a terrible skin disease called leprosy. People with leprosy had a hard life. Not only did they have sores on their skin, but they were not allowed to be around anyone else. Healthy people were afraid of catching the disease too. So lepers, as those with the illness were called, had to live in colonies outside town, away from everyone else. They were poor and lonely people.

Jesus saw the ten lepers and told them to go show their skin to the priests. The priests were the only ones who could say that a person was cured of leprosy and was allowed to be with healthy people again.

On their way to see the priests, the men noticed that their skin was healed. The sores were gone. Their skin was smooth and clear. Nine of the men rushed on to see the priest so that they could be declared healed and begin living a normal life again.

But one man, when he saw that he was healed, came back to Jesus, praising God all the way. He knelt down in front of Jesus and thanked him for the gift of health.

The one man in the story realized that the gift of healing came from God. All good gifts come from God, who deserves our thanks and our praise.

Let's Pray. Dear God, we thank you for the many good gifts you give to us. May we never take the blessings of our lives for granted but always offer you the thanks and praise you deserve. In Jesus' name we pray. Amen.

Waiting For God's Answer

Prop Needed
A glass of water

The Message
One time a little boy named Timmy was having a hard time getting to sleep.* He called downstairs to his dad and asked for a drink of water. (*Hold up glass.*) His father called back up to Timmy, "You already had a drink. Now go to sleep!"

Timmy said, "But Daddy, I'm still thirsty! Please may I have another drink of water?"

"No!" his father answered.

A few minutes went by before Timmy's voice drifted down the stairs again. "Daddy, please, I'm really, really thirsty!"

But Timmy's father thought he just wanted to stay up longer, so he said, "For the last time, no! And if I hear another word about it, I'm coming up there and giving you a spanking!"

There was a pause, and then the father heard Timmy say, "When you come up to give me a spanking, could you please bring a glass of water with you?"

Timmy's father then knew that his boy was honestly thirsty and took him a drink, with no spanking.

Jesus told his disciples not to give up praying if God didn't give them what they wanted right away. God does hear our prayers and answers them. Sometimes we don't have to wait long for the answers. God gives us a pretty quick yes or no to our prayers. We either get what we've asked for or we don't.

*Based on an anecdote published in *Pulpit Helps* magazine.

Other times God's answer to our prayers is, "Wait." Maybe it isn't the right time for you to have what you've asked for. Or maybe what we've asked for isn't really what you want at all, and God is giving you time to figure that out.

There's a story about a girl named Julie. Julie's parents decided they weren't happy living together anymore, and so they were going to get a divorce. Julie's dad moved to an apartment, and Julie was very sad. Every night she prayed that her parents would get back together again.

Finally, after months of waiting and praying, the final papers were signed. Julie's parents were divorced. Julie felt angry and betrayed by God. She longed for things to be the way they used to be. But then she started to think back to how things really were. She remembered bitter arguments, slamming doors, and cold silences in her home during the last couple of years her parents lived together. Julie realized that an angry family wasn't what she wanted either. What she really wanted most was for her parents to be happy and to feel loved by each of them. Then she realized that her prayer was already answered.

Let's Pray. God, we know that when we pray, you hear us, and you answer us. Help us to be patient, if we need to wait for your answer. In Jesus' name we pray. Amen.

TWENTY-THIRD SUNDAY AFTER   Proper 25
PENTECOST   Prayer and Justification
Luke 18:9–14

The Minister and the Thief

Props Needed
Flannel board
Flannel-board figures (found in the Appendix)

The Message

Once there were two men who went to a church to pray. One man was a minister. (*Put minister figure on the flannel board.*) The other man was a thief. (*Put thief figure on the flannel board.*)

The minister walked down the center aisle of the church with his head held high. He was carrying a Bible in his hand. When he came to the end of the aisle, he looked up to the stained glass window of Jesus and began to pray.

"I thank you, God, that I am not greedy and dishonest, like everybody else. I thank you that I am not like that thief over there. I come to church, even on my time off, I do volunteer work at the soup kitchen downtown, and I give a generous share of my money to the church." The minister felt quite proud of himself, and was sure that he had earned God's love.

When the thief came into the church, he walked down the side aisle, looking at the floor. He slid into a pew, and knelt down. He didn't even look up at the stained glass window of Jesus. He simply said, very quietly, "God forgive me, because I am a sinner."

Which of these two men do you think pleased God more, the minister or the thief? How many of you think the minister? Raise your hands. How many of you think the thief? Why? (*Listen to reasons.*)

Jesus told a story a lot like this one. He said the thief was the one who made God more happy. Why? Because God's love cannot be earned or bought. The minister thought that he could make God love him by doing good deeds and giving money to the church. But no matter how hard we try, we will never be good enough to earn or deserve God's love. God doesn't love us because we deserve it. God loves us because of who God is.

The thief understood that. He knew he didn't deserve God's love. He knew he must depend on God to forgive him his mistakes and love him anyway.

God loves all of us, even though we aren't perfect. God wants us to try our best to be good people, but not as a way to get the Lord to love us. The Lord already loves us. We do good deeds and try to be the best we can be as a way of thanking God for that love and forgiveness.

Let's Pray. Dear God, we know that we do not deserve your love. But you love us anyway. Thank you for such a special gift. In Jesus' name we pray. Amen.

Making a Change

Props Needed
Flannel board
Flannel-board figures (found in the Appendix)

The Message
Have you ever been in a large crowd of people, wanting to see something, but unable to see it because everyone else was taller than you—perhaps at a parade or at the monkey house at the zoo? If you're behind a large group of people, you can't see what's going on, can you? What do you do at a time like that? (*Listen to answers.*)

The same thing happened a long time ago to a man named Zacchaeus. The Bible tells us that Jesus was passing through a town called Jericho. (*Have tree and house in place on flannel board. Follow story with figures.*) Zacchaeus was a tax collector in Jericho.

The people hated tax collectors because they cheated them. Zacchaeus heard about Jesus and wanted to see him. Many other people came out of their homes and shops to see Jesus too. There were so many people lining the streets that Zacchaeus couldn't see a thing. He was very short. No one would let him get to the front of the crowd to see, because he was a tax collector.

Zacchaeus had an idea. He saw a sycamore tree down the street. He ran to the tree and climbed it. From high in the tree he had a perfect view of Jesus. He was not expecting what happened next, though. Jesus stopped right under the tree and looked up at Zacchaeus. He said, "Come on down out of that tree, Zacchaeus. Tonight I'm having supper with you at your house."

Zacchaeus was very happy. He jumped out of the tree and took Jesus to his home. The rest of the crowd was very angry. They couldn't understand why Jesus would choose to visit such a bad person.

But Jesus knew what he was doing. When they got to Zacchaeus's house, the tax collector said to Jesus, "Listen, sir! I will give away half of what I own to the poor. And if I have ever cheated any people, I will pay them back four times what I owe them!"

Jesus' visit made Zacchaeus realize that he was wrong to cheat people. He decided to turn over a new leaf, as we say. He was going to change his life and become a better, more honest person. He promised to give to the poor and pay back those he had cheated.

Jesus went to Zacchaeus's house because he knew the tax collector needed him most. Jesus helped Zacchaeus change his life for the better. Jesus has that effect on people. He makes us want to be the best people we can be. And then he helps us do it.

Let's Pray. Dear God, sometimes it is easy to judge other people and to say, "Oh, he's not very nice" or "She's really a pain." Help us to look for the good in others instead of seeing only the bad. In Jesus' name we pray. Amen.

TWENTY-FIFTH SUNDAY AFTER   Proper 27
PENTECOST   Death and Resurrection
Luke 20:27–38

The Seasons of Life

Prop Needed
An autumn leaf

The Message

Autumn is a pretty time of the year. The air feels clean and crisp. Crunchy apples are in season. And the prettiest part is the colors of the leaves—gold and orange and red. In autumn the leaves change colors and then fall to the ground, don't they? I found this leaf in my yard this morning. We have a lot of trees in our yard. Several weeks ago I raked the leaves into a huge pile. My children loved playing in the big piles of leaves. (*Of course, you'll need to adapt this part of the story to your circumstances. It could be your neighbor with the leaves and children playing in them, your own grandchildren playing, or something you enjoyed doing as a child.*) How many of you like to play in big piles of leaves?

I like autumn, but a part of me feels a little sad this time of the year. When the leaves on the trees change colors, they're beautiful. But when the leaves all fall off, the trees look kind of bare, don't they? The trees even look dead without their leaves. And they stay that way for months, all through the winter—bare, dead-looking trees.

I would be really sad and worried, thinking about the dead-looking trees, except for one thing. I know that in springtime, beautiful, new leaves will grow on the trees. Some trees will even have flowers blooming on their branches!

All living things must die. Some of you may have had a pet, or a friend, or a relative who died. When someone dies we feel sad.

We know we won't see that person again as long as we live. We will miss that person. We will miss doing things and being together.

But just as the trees grow new leaves in spring, God promises new life for those who love the Lord. God promises us heaven. What that means is, when our bodies don't work anymore, they die, like the old leaves. But our souls, the part of us that makes us who we are, our souls go to live forever with God.

So when someone we love dies, we are sad because we'll miss that person. We may even be angry at him or her for leaving us. But we can also be happy, because we know that he or she is in a good place, with God. We will see that person again someday when we are all together in God's springtime, which is heaven.

Let's Pray. Dear God, you give us life, and then you promise us new life with you in heaven. Thank you for these priceless gifts. In the name of the One who makes these gifts possible, even Jesus we pray. Amen.

Whose Side Are You On?

Prop Needed

A superheroes comic book

The Message

Do any of you like to read comic books? I brought one with me this morning. It's called *(name of book)*. *(Hero's name)* is the good guy, or hero, of this comic book. In the story, . . . *(describe the story up to the climax)*. It's a pretty exciting story. Who do you think is going to win in the end? *(Listen to answers.)*

In comic books, the forces of good and evil often battle one another—it's the good folks against the bad folks. If the bad folks win, if evil wins, the world is doomed for sure. If the good folks win, the world is saved . . . at least until the next comic book comes out with another evil villain who tries to take over the world. Almost every time, the hero or heroine triumphs over evil by the end of the comic book story.

The forces of good and evil battle each other in the real world too. Sometimes it's hard to figure out which side is winning.

If you listen to the news on TV, you hear terrible reports about wars, people robbing or murdering each other, people without a home or enough food to eat, child abuse—all kinds of things that make you think maybe the bad folks are winning.

But then we see so many good things in our world too. People unselfishly helping others, friends and family who love us, people working to find cures for diseases like cancer, beautiful paintings and music, a rainbow—all kinds of things that make us think maybe good is going to triumph over evil after all.

We don't need to worry about whether good or evil is going to win the struggle in our world. We already know. The Lord has already told us the end of the story. God is going to win in the end, which of course means that when all is said and done, good will triumph over evil. When that happens, all people will live together in peace. There will be no more wars, no more crime, no more diseases, no more hurt feelings. Everything will be the way God wanted it to be all along.

People have been waiting for this miracle to happen for thousands and thousands of years. No one knows when the war between good and evil will be over and God declared the winner. Until that does happen it is our job as Christians to do all we can to help good win over evil. Be kind to one another. Be honest and unselfish. Help others. Choose to be on God's side.

Let's Pray. Dear God, there are many difficult things in our world that we have to deal with. Help us to face the hard things with courage and faith. Amen.

Who's in Charge?

Props Needed
A dollar bill
A picture of the current United States president

The message

Can anyone tell me whose picture is on the one dollar bill? (*Show the children the bill, and pause for answers.*) It's George Washington. George Washington must have been pretty important to have his face on the dollar bill. Who was George Washington? (*Pause for answers.*) That's right, he was the first president of our country, the United States of America. That is important, isn't it?

The president is the head of our country. He or she is the single most important leader in our government.

You knew that George Washington was the first president, but who is the president of the United States now? (*Pause for answers.*) It's (*name of current president*) (*Name*) doesn't run the country alone, but if you had to name one person in charge of the United States, it would be (*name of the president*).

Do you know who is the head of the church? Who is in charge? (*Pause for answers.*) No, not (*your pastor's name*). She's the pastor and an important leader, but the head of the church is Jesus.

Jesus is the single most important leader in the church—and not only in our church here in (*your town and state*), but in all Christian churches everywhere in the world.

When Jesus was born, many people expected him to be a king. How many of you know how to play "King of the Hill"? One person, the king, stands on top of a hill. The other players try to run up and push the king off the hill and take his or her place. At the same time, the king tries to push and shove everyone else back down the hill.

This was the kind of king some people wanted Jesus to be. They wanted him to charge up the hill, shove the Romans, who were in power, out of the way, and take over. Jesus refused to be that kind of leader. He told people that his leadership would be something different and totally unexpected. And it is.

Jesus showed us power and authority come from God, not from having the most guns or jets or bombs. Jesus is our leader, because we are part of his church. He is the most dependable, trustworthy, and most important leader in our lives.

Let's Pray. Dear God, help us to listen to Jesus, our leader and our friend, and to be good citizens in God's world. Amen.

Appendix

To Prepare Flannel-board Figures

Cut the pages containing the needed flannel-board figures out of the book. Glue the page onto a piece of stiff cardboard, such as the cardboard that comes with a new shirt. Cut around the outline of each figure. Color the figures, using crayons, marking pens, or colored pencils. Glue small squares of medium-grade sandpaper to the top, bottom, and middle of each figure.

Jesus

disciples

women

Thomas

Doubting Thomas
(pages 68–69)

All People Created Equal
(pages 90–91)

"People with leprosy"

"Jesus"

On Giving Thanks
(pages 124–25)

The Minister and the Thief
(pages 128–29)

"Jesus"

"Zacchaeus"

"Crowd"

"angry people"

Making a Change
(page 130-31)

To Make Flannel Board

Cut a piece of masonite or foam board to the desired size. Using powder-blue flannel four inches larger than the board (Diagram 1), pull the flannel to the back of the board, being sure it is smooth and taut on the front. Glue or tape the corners of the flannel to the back of the board first (Diagram 2). Then glue or tape the top and bottom edges (Diagram 3), and finally the side edges (Diagram 4).

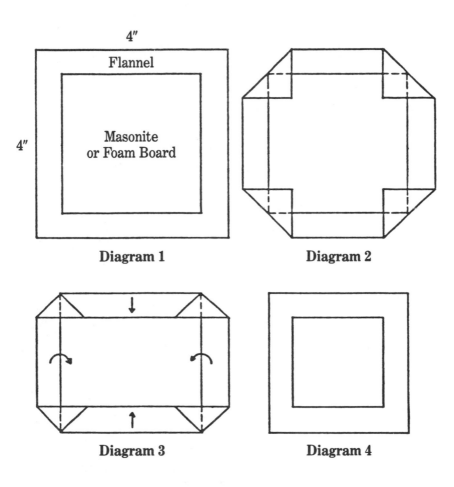

4"

4"

Flannel

Masonite or Foam Board

Diagram 1

Diagram 2

Diagram 3

Diagram 4

Indexes

Scripture Index

Topical Index